WADSWORTH PHILOSOPHERS SERIES

ON

CAMUS

Richard Kamber
The College of New Jersey

D1568311

WADSWORTH

THOMSON LEARNING

Australia • Canada • Mexico • Singapore • Spain
United Kingdom • United States

WADSWORTH

TM

THOMSON LEARNING

To my father, William Kamber,
and a few gifted teachers,
who taught me to love words and ideas

Printed in the United States of America
1 2 3 4 5 6 7 04 03 02 01

For permission to use material from this text, contact us:
Web: http://www.thomsonrights.com
Fax: 1-800-730-2215
Phone: 1-800-730-2214

For more information, contact:
Wadsworth/Thomson Learning, Inc.
10 Davis Drive
Belmont, CA 94002-3098
USA
http://www.wadsworth.com

ISBN: 0-534-58381-4

CONTENTS

PREFACE

I have written *On Camus* to provide a philosophical overview of Albert Camus' work. While this book may be of interest to Camus scholars, it is intended primarily as a guide for readers who want to examine what is philosophically important in Camus' works but lack an extensive background in philosophy or familiarity with all of Camus' principal publications. Thus, the design of this book presupposes only a willingness to read, think, and learn. Since *On Camus* is a short book, it emphasizes what Camus himself had to say rather than what critics have had to say about him. Where possible, I have taken quotations from standard English translations. Where necessary for reasons of precision or availability, I have used my own translations.

As Pierre Grouix noted, "one does not write about Camus as a philosopher without discomfort" (Grouix, 65). Although Camus' works are filled with attempts to express philosophical issues and ideas, these attempts are sometimes unclear or illogical. If Camus had had the benefit of more formal education in philosophy, or if he had been less interested in philosophical issues, then the task of understanding the philosophical import of his work would probably be easier. As matters stand, it is not easy, and most of the books and articles written about Camus lack philosophical precision.

Chapter 1 of this book is a compact summary of Camus' life and work. Chapter 2 examines the religious roots of Camus' philosophical thought with particular attention to his graduate thesis *Christian Metaphysics and Neoplatonism*. Chapters 3 and 4 analyze and criticize his trilogy on the absurd: *The Stranger*, *Caligula*, and *The Myth of Sisyphus*. Chapter 5 examines Camus' development as a moralist in *Letters to a German Friend*, *The Plague*, *The Rebel*, and *The Fall*.

1
Life and Works

Albert Camus was born in Mondovi, Algeria on November 8, 1913. His father, Lucien, an orphan who had taught himself how to read, worked as a cellarman in a nearby winery. His mother, Catherine Hélène Sintès, was illiterate and suffered from speech and hearing defects. Both parents were children of poor Europeans who had settled in Algeria in hopes of finding better opportunities than they had at home. His father's family had come from France; his mother's from the Spanish island of Minorca. Eight months after Albert's birth, his father was mobilized for military service in World War I. Dressed in the dashing red and blue uniform of the First Zouave Regiment, he made an easy target for German machine guns. In September 1914, he was wounded by a shell in the Battle of the Marne and died a few weeks later. All Albert knew of his father were some family stories.

Camus' boyhood in Algiers was a mixture of harsh poverty and simple pleasures. He lived in a cramped three-room apartment with his mother, brother, grandmother, and two uncles. They had neither electricity nor running water. On the landing were Turkish toilets—holes with drains that stank constantly. His mother worked as a cleaning woman. His grandmother, who was also illiterate, ran the family and used a whip to discipline the boys. Yet Albert adored his mother and enjoyed the company of his brothers and uncles. He loved the beach, the sea, and the sun. He enjoyed the street life of children in the Belcourt district, on the edge of the Arab quarter. In his last work,

1

an unfinished, autobiographical novel called *The First Man*, Camus stresses the casual attitude of his family toward religion. While nominally Catholics, they had little use for priests, and did not attend mass or talk about God. "They were Catholics as they were French; it entailed a certain number of rituals. . . . baptism, First Communion, marriage . . . and funeral rites" (Camus, *FM*, 1995, 165).

A critical figure in Camus' life was a primary school teacher named Louis Germain. Germain recognized Albert's abilities and persuaded the boy's grandmother to permit him to tutor her grandson for a scholarship competition. She agreed, and Albert won the scholarship that enabled him to go to high school instead of going to work like his brother. In high school, Camus found another mentor: a talented philosophy teacher named Jean Grenier. Of the many books Camus read during his high school, the two he admired most were Grenier's *Islands* (*Les Iles*) and André Malraux's *Man's Fate* (*La Condition humaine.*) In 1959, Camus wrote that *Islands* had compensated for his lack of traditional religious training by reminding him of "mystery . . . holy things . . . the finite nature of man" (Camus, *LCE*, 1970, 328). Camus also learned from *Islands* how to suggest philosophical ideas by describing concrete things and events.

During his first year in high school, Camus was diagnosed with tuberculosis, a disease that would plague him throughout his life. Antibiotics had not yet been discovered, but treatments of lung collapse therapy allowed him to recover from incapacitating bouts of this disease. In 1933, Camus entered the University of Algiers to earn a graduate diploma in philosophy. He wrote a thesis entitled *Christian Metaphysics and Neoplatonism* (*Métaphysique Chrétienne et Néoplatonisme*). Although his grades were not outstanding, they qualified him to apply for doctoral study (*agrégation*) and certification as a philosophy professor. Then, in 1938, his application was rejected by the Surgeon General of Algeria. The government did not want to run the risk of paying medical care for an invalid.

Camus' mix of confidence and vulnerability, his stylish clothes, and soulful good looks (he resembled Humphrey Bogart) made him a great success with women. Yet at age 20, he rushed into marriage with a dazzling bohemian, Simone Hié. Simone's mother, a successful ophthalmologist, supported the couple generously in the hope that Camus could help Simone break her drug habit. He could not. When he discovered that she was having sex with a doctor in exchange for drugs, they separated. In 1940, Camus married again. His second wife

2

was Francine Faure, a mathematics teacher from Oran. She too was beautiful, but private and reserved. In 1945, Francine gave birth to twins: Catherine and Jean. Although never divorced, Francine suffered immensely from Albert's persistent and public infidelities.

In the mid-1930's, Camus was brimming with energy. He became a journalist for *Alger Républicain*, wrote a novel, essays and plays, ran theatre groups, and joined the Communist Party. His career as a Communist was short-lived. In 1937, the Party expelled him for supporting Arab radicals in their bid for social and civil rights. But Camus' career as a writer was just beginning. His first novel, *A Happy Death* (*La Mort heureuse*), lacked sufficient unity to merit publication, but he published a collection of essays entitled *The Wrong Side and the Right Side* (*L'Envers et l'endroit*) in 1937 and a second collection, called *Nuptials* (*Noces*), in 1939.

The year 1939 also marked the start of World War II. Camus tried to enlist in the army, but was rejected because of his health. In the spring of 1940, the German army overwhelmed France. The liberal *Alger Républicain* was soon banned, and Camus found himself in need of work. His friend Pascal Pia helped him get a job in Paris doing layouts for *Paris-Soir*. In 1942, Camus published a remarkable novel *The Stranger* (*L'Etranger*), followed in 1943 by a related collection of essays *The Myth of Sisyphus* (*Le Mythe de Sisyphe*). Recognition as an author helped him win an editorial post with his new publisher, Gallimard. He would continue working with Gallimard until his death.

Camus hated every thing about the Nazis. He hated their racism, anti-Semitism, totalitarianism, and taste for cold-blooded murder. He joined the French Resistance in 1943 and soon became editor of a clandestine newspaper called *Combat*. In 1944-1945, Camus produced and published two powerful plays: *The Misunderstanding* (*Le Malentendu*) and *Caligula*. He also became friends with Jean-Paul Sartre (1905-1980), Simone de Beauvoir (1908-1986), and other members of their circle. For a man born into a world of poverty and illiteracy, it was an exhilarating and somewhat intimidating experience to be at the center of the Parisian intellectual scene.

It was during the Nazi Occupation of France that Camus' name first became linked with existentialism. Although the French word *'existentialiste'* seems to have been coined about 1943 by Gabriel Marcel (1889-1973), a Catholic philosopher, the idea of a philosophy focused on issues of human existence, choice, and authenticity can be traced back to Søren Kierkegaard (1813-1855), a passionate Protestant.

Camus was keenly interested in existential issues and deeply influenced by two thinkers associated with the formation of existentialism: Fyodor Dostoyevsky (1821-1881) and Friedrich Nietzsche (1844-1900). Yet Camus always refused to label himself an existentialist. At first, he refused because he identified existentialism with a religious leap of faith. Later, he refused because he identified existentialism with the philosophy of Jean-Paul Sartre.

The end of World War II brought Camus an international audience and a chance to participate in the rebuilding of France. For four years he struggled to clarify the moral and political lessons he had learned from fighting Nazi tyranny in editorials, *Letters to a German Friend (Lettres à un ami allemand*, 1945), "Neither Victims nor Executioners" (*"Ni Victimes ni bourreaux*," 1946), his second novel *The Plague (La Peste*, 1947) and a play entitled *State of Siege (L'Etat de siège*, 1948).

By 1948, the Cold War had overshadowed the alliances of World War II. Camus' 1949 play *The Just Assassins (Les Justes)* and his 1951 treatise *The Rebel (L'Homme révolté)* dealt with issues of revolt, revolution, and tyranny. Camus argued that Marxism and the Soviet Union posed a greater threat to human freedom, dignity, and happiness than Western capitalism. At about the same time, Sartre arrived at contrary conclusions. After a bitter exchange of public letters, their friendship ended. Camus had already lost the friendship of Pascal Pia, who now supported Charles de Gaulle and his centrist party.

In 1954, Camus published a short collection of essays under the title *Summer (L'Eté)*. Although written at different times, they reflected Camus' love of Algeria and the Mediterranean spirit. Unfortunately, the harmony of that spirit was about to be broken.

In October 1954, a revolutionary organization, the National Liberation Front (FLN) began attacks on European Algerians (settlers or *pieds-noirs*). In 1955, the French military retaliated against FLN massacres with indiscriminate bloodshed based on a policy of "collective responsibility." During the battle of Algiers, the French used torture to intimidate prisoners and extract information. Sartre and his "family" sided with the FLN rebels who wanted to liberate Algeria from France. Camus was torn. He despised the racism that relegated over eight million native Algerians to second-class citizenship. But he deplored the violence of the FLN and recognized that an FLN "liberation" of Algeria would probably result in the exodus of over a million non-Arab Algerians—including members of his own family. "I believe in justice," he said, "but I will defend my mother before justice" (Todd, 378). He campaigned for a civilian truce, endorsed Algerian autonomy within a French federation, and went to Algeria to gather supporters. When neither side found his views realistic, he lapsed into silence for two years. In 1962, Algeria gained full independence, and most of the European population fled in panic to southern France.

In 1956, Camus published his third novel *The Fall* (*La Chute*). It was noticeably different in style and message from anything he had written before. Reviews were mixed, but the book sold 126,500 copies in its first six months. The following year he published an impressive collection of short stories under the title *Exile and the Kingdom* (*L'Exile et le royaume*) and an essay against capital punishment called "Reflections on the Guillotine" ("*Réflexions sur la guillotine*).

In 1957, Camus was awarded the Nobel Prize for Literature. This should have been a joy and triumph for Camus, but his happiness was marred by worries. He was worried about his worthiness to receive this honor and said repeatedly that the prize should have gone to André Malraux. He was worried about Francine's depressions and suicidal behavior and his own declining health. He was worried about the turmoil in Algeria, his estrangement from other French intellectuals, and his capacity to continue producing works of quality. At age 43, he feared his best years were behind him. He told one reporter: "The Nobel gave me the sudden feeling of being old" (Todd, 381).

Throughout his life, Camus had enjoyed adapting and producing the works of other authors for the stage. As early as 1936, he had staged a play based on Malraux's novel *Days of Wrath* (*Le Temps de mépris*). As recently as 1956, he had produced an adaptation of William Faulkner's *Requiem for a Nun*. In 1959, Camus wrote and produced an adaptation of Dostoyevky's *The Possessed*. He thought about devoting ten years of his life to the theater. But Camus' highest hopes were invested in his autobiographical novel *The First Man*.

Between book royalties and Nobel Prize money, Camus was rich. He began looking for a larger apartment in Paris and bought a handsome stone farmhouse for his family in Provence. (Mi, Camus' young, Danish mistress often stayed at a farmhouse nearby.) Far from the lights of Paris, Camus found more time to work on *The First Man*. He believed it would be his finest novel and dedicated it to his mother. It reads: "To you who will never be able to read this book" (Camus, *FM*, 1996, 3). The 144-page manuscript contains no explicit philosophy, but it offers fresh insights into Camus' understanding of his moral education. He writes, for example, that as a child he tried to discover the difference between right and wrong but no one could tell him. "And now that everything is leaving me I realize I need someone to show me the way and to blame me and praise me, by right not of power but of authority, I need my father" (Camus, *FM*, 1996, 36).

On January 3, 1960, Camus left his country home with Michel and Janine Gallimard, their daughter Anne and the family dog for a two-day drive back to Paris. Michel was driving the next day when the car swerved off the road, struck two trees, and broke into pieces. Camus was killed instantly. Michel died a few days later. Janine and Anne were unhurt. The dog disappeared. Camus had often said to friends that there was nothing more scandalous than the death of a child, and nothing more absurd than to die in a car accident. When word reached Camus' mother in Algiers that her son was dead, she was not able to weep. "Too young" she said. (Todd, 414).

A few days after Camus' death, Sartre wrote a generous obituary which dwelt on the cruel absurdity of an eloquent voice silenced in mid-career and praised Camus as "the present heir of that long line of moralists whose work perhaps constitute what is most original in French letters" (Sartre 1965, 110-111). This identification of Camus as a "*moraliste*" in the tradition of Montaigne, Pascal, Voltaire and others seems precisely right. Camus' genius lay in his frequent success in addressing the moral intelligence of his readers by embodying philosophical ideas in literary form. This success is most evident in his three novels and in some of his essays, including "The Myth of Sisyphus." Other works are less successful. At times, Camus' philosophical ideas exceeded his grasp of the relevant issues or his skill at giving them literary expression.

Camus often denied that he was a philosopher, and most critics have taken him at his word. Yet Camus' denials were based more on differences in method than differences in subject matter. He wrote to Francine: "I don't believe in thoughts expressed during discussions or in the clash of ideas. I am not a philosopher, and for me thought is an interior adventure that matures, that hurts or transports one" (Todd, 280). Camus wanted his philosophical thinking to arise from lived experience and to remain tempered by observation and moral feelings. He was distrustful of unfettered reason and system making. He sought to philosophize in ways that were compatible with the conversations of humankind, continuous with the preoccupations of religion, and capable of being expressed without special terminology.

2

The Religious Roots of Camus' Philosophical Thought

A. "Christian Preoccupations"

A few days after receiving the Nobel Prize for literature, Camus remarked during an interview: "I have Christian preoccupations, but my nature is pagan" (Camus, *Essais*, 1965, 1615). What were Camus' preoccupations? As a philosophical thinker, he was preoccupied with questions about the place of humanity in the universe, the meaning of human life, reasons for living, and morality—questions central to all religions, including Christianity. Unlike Sartre and most professional philosophers of his time, he was not particularly interested in questions about consciousness, perception, knowledge, free will, or being. Thus, he was correct in saying that he shared the preoccupation of Christians. But Camus was not a Christian. He neither believed in God nor accepted the specific morality of Christianity. He liked to think of himself as instinctively pagan: a man in love with the tangible pleasures of this earth rather than the ethereal blessings of heaven. Like Sisyphus in "The Myth of Sisyphus," he preferred "water and sun, warm stones and sea" to rewards for divine obedience (Camus, *Myth*, 1955, 8).

7

Camus was also pagan in his preference for the openness and moderation of a "Greek" outlook over—what he took to be—the absolutism of Christianity. In an earlier interview, he said:

> I am not Christian. I was born poor, under a happy sky, in an environment with which one felt accord, not hostility. . . . But I feel that I have a Greek heart . . . . the Greeks did not deny their gods, *but they only gave them their portion.* Christianity is a total religion . . . (Camus *Essais,* 1965, 380).

Camus' philosophical thought is deeply rooted in religious issues. To comprehend and evaluate that thought, it is necessary to be familiar, not only with the issues themselves, but also with the particular philosophers and writers who helped to shape his understanding of these issues. Yet his best known works seldom mention by name the religious thinkers who contributed most to his early development.

In *The Myth of Sisyphus,* for example, Camus insists that the "facts" regarding the absurd are well known and that he is mainly interested in exploring the consequences. He writes: "Let me repeat: all this has been said over and over. . . . They run through all literatures and philosophies. Everyday conversation feeds on them" (Camus *Myth,* 1955, 12). But Camus exaggerates when he says, "they run through all literatures and philosophies." Most writers and philosophers have concluded that *on balance* the world is *not* absurd. Moreover, some philosophers (e.g. Spinoza, Leibniz, and Hegel) have argued that the world is not absurd at all. Who are the authors Camus has in mind? They are not *all* authors, but authors he found especially interesting, at least in part, because of their worries about the world's real or apparent absurdity. Consequently, it is helpful in analyzing Camus' writings to identify some of the key sources that formed the background of his thought and impelled him to explore issues such as the consequences of living in an absurd world. Among the most important were the God-centered philosophers discussed below.

B. Blaise Pascal

In 1934, when Camus was just twenty-one, he wrote to his friend, Claude de Fréminville about his admiration for Blaise Pascal. He said: "If you knew how ravishing Pascal is . . . clear, profound, and unforgettable about the human heart and in his despairing glory" (Todd, 30). In some respects, Camus' admiration for Pascal might seem odd. Pascal was a seventeenth century scientific and mathematical genius who devoted the last years of his life to defending Christianity. Camus had little interest in science or mathematics and rejected Christianity. On the other hand, Pascal was a brilliant essayist with deep psychological and philosophical insights. His most famous book, the *Pensées*, was written for worldly and educated people who, like Camus, were skeptical about religion or regarded it as a matter of little personal importance. Pascal knew what it meant to see the world from the vantage point of reason without appeal to faith or religious teachings. He knew how to get the attention of people who preferred to live without such appeals. Although Camus was not persuaded by Pascal's religious conclusions, he was fascinated by his vision of the human condition and the challenges he posed to people who wanted to forgo the comforts of religion.

Pascal's overall strategy in the *Pensées* can be understood as a five-part argument. First, he wants to convince readers who feel confident about the capacity of the human intellect to understand and cope with the world that their confidence is misplaced. He argues that neither reason, science, nor the institutions of society (government, professions, etc.) are dependable guides to reality or happiness. He declares that our deepest intuitions do not come from reason: "The heart has its reasons, which reason doesn't know" (Pascal 1958, 78). Second, Pascal wants to demonstrate that the human condition without a personal commitment to a merciful God and hope of eternal salvation is a condition of misery. He argues that human beings are driven by boredom and vanity to seek petty triumphs and hollow honors while neglecting what should matter most to them: the inevitability of death and the possibility of eternal life. Third, Pascal wants to show that, while reason can neither prove nor disprove the existence of God, it can prove that we would be fools not to bet on the chance that there is a merciful God. This is his famous "wager." Finally, Pascal tries to establish that if one is going to bet on God, there is overwhelming evidence that one should embrace God as taught by Christianity. He argues at great length that Christianity offers an account of human history and humanity's relationship with God that is more powerful, consistent, and comprehensive than that offered by any other religion.

One of Pascal's most original views is his theory of diversion (*divertissement*). He proposes this theory to explain the seemingly absurd tendency of human beings to neglect, risk, or even sacrifice their enduring interests for the sake of a little glory or a bit of excitement. In a particularly famous fragment of the *Pensées*, he writes:

> I have discovered that all of the unhappiness of men arises from one single fact, that they cannot stay quietly in their own chamber. A man who has enough to live on, if he knew how to stay with pleasure at home, would not leave it to go to sea or besiege a town. . . . But on further consideration, when, after finding the same cause of all our ills, I have sought to discover the reason of it, I have found that there is one very real reason for it, namely, the natural poverty of our feeble and mortal condition, so miserable that nothing can comfort us when we think of it closely (Pascal 1958, 39).

What Pascal is claiming is that a great deal of human behavior is motivated unconsciously by a desire to avoid thinking about how feeble our lives are and how close we are to death. Although he acknowledges that other motives, such as boredom, vanity, and longing for contentment also enter into our choices, he is eager to reveal the unseen role played by our desire for diversion.

Pascal's theory of diversion permeates Camus' thought. Like Pascal, Camus believes that most people fail to recognize the absurdity of the human condition because they are adept at self-deception: they live within a "stage set." The chief difference, of course, is that Camus regards religion as a form of self-deception and diversion.

Camus is also indebted to Pascal for his vivid depiction of the incomprehensibility of the universe and the certainty of death. Note, for example, how Pascal makes his vision of the world personal:

> I know not who put me into the world, nor what the world is, nor what I myself am. I am in terrible ignorance of everything. . . . I see nothing but infinities on all sides . . . All I know is that I must die soon, but what I know least is this very death which I cannot escape (Pascal 1958, 55).

In another fragment, Pascal compares the human condition to that of condemned prisoners.

> Let us imagine a number of men in chains, and all condemned

10

to death, where some are killed each day in the sight of the others, and those who remain see their fate in that of their fellows, and wait their turn, looking at each other sorrowfully and without hope. It is an image of the condition of men (Pascal 1958, 60).

Camus returns repeatedly to this image of condemned prisoners. It is Meursault at the end of *The Stranger* recognizing that his condition as a condemned prisoner is not fundamentally different from the destiny of every human being since: "one destiny alone must elect me, and with me billions of privileged people . . . The others would all be condemned one day" (Camus, *TRN*, 1962, 1208-1209). It is also the mad emperor in *Caligula* transforming Rome into death row:

> "A man dies because he is guilty. A man is guilty because he is one of Caligula's subjects. Now all men are Caligula's subjects. Ergo, all men are guilty and shall die. It is only a matter of time and patience" (Camus, CTOP, 1962, 29).

Death row is also a dominant image in Camus' novel, *The Plague*. In this novel, the city of Oran on Algeria's Mediterranean coast is stricken by bubonic plague and placed under quarantine. The citizens of Oran are imprisoned in their own city, where hundreds are killed each day by a faceless executioner, crueler and more capricious than Caligula, and those who remain wonder when their turn will come. In *The Rebel*, Camus argues that historical revolutions draw their logic and themes from "metaphysical rebellion" against the human condition— especially against "the mass death sentence" that defines the human condition (Camus, *Rebel*, 1956, 24).

Although Camus shares Pascal's bleak vision of humanity's alienation and mortality in the natural world, he does not share the lesson that Pascal draws from this vision. Pascal argues that the only reasonable course to take in the face of the human condition is to bet on the possibility that there is a merciful God who will grant us eternal life if we reach out to Him in all sincerity. Pascal readily admits that reason can neither prove nor disprove such a God, but he argues that we have everything to gain and nothing to lose by making this wager. If you bet on God (conceived in this way) and He exists, then you will gain an eternity of happiness. If you bet on God and He does not exist, you will still acquire important virtues and give up nothing but

11

negligible pleasures. If you bet against this God and He does not exist, you will gain nothing for having guessed right. If you bet against this God and He exists, you will lose an eternity of happiness and perhaps face an eternity of suffering.

Pascal's wager is not a stand-alone argument, but a link in a chain of arguments forged in the fragments of the *Pensées*. It is anchored on one end by Pascal's interpretation of the human condition—the misery of man without God—and on the other end by his understanding of what is involved in wagering on God, his conception of divine grace, and his arguments for the reasonableness and explanatory power of Christianity. For example, it has been objected that God might reserve the lowest circle of hell as punishment for those who choose to believe in him simply as a matter of a wager. But this objection makes sense only if wagering on God is understood to be a casual bet, a cynical affirmation without real conviction. As Pascal makes clear, his idea of wagering on God is very far from being casual or cynical. What he has in mind is an existential choice of a way of life in which religion plays a central role.

Pascal's own commitment to Christianity was based on the influence of his family and personal experience and not on the wager. His father and sister, Jacqueline, were active members of a Catholic sect called Jansenism that held very strict views on what was required for salvation. On the night of November 23, 1654, Pascal had a profound religious experience. The experience was so important to him that he wrote a "Memorial" about it, which he carried with him until his death, sewn into his clothes. It said, in part: "God of Abraham, God of Isaac, God of Jacob, not of the philosophers and scholars. Certainty, certainty, heartfelt joy, peace. God of Jesus Christ . . Everlasting joy in return for one day's effort on earth" (Pascal 1995, 285-286).

Although this talk of Pascal's personal revelation may seem remote from Camus' resolute denial of God, it is not. Pascal haunted Camus as a spokesman for a Christian point-of-view that Camus could not dismiss as naïve, inconsistent, or philosophically suicidal. Pascal believed that he *knew* the truth of Christianity with as much certainty as anything could possibly be known. He also believed that most people did not have this kind of certainty and, therefore, needed to be coaxed by various arguments into taking the path of faith.

What could Camus say to Pascal? An answer to this question is suggested by a number of statements that he made in 1945 on ministering to the damned. In a January 1945 issue of *Combat*, he responded to the arguments of the Catholic novelist François Mauriac (1885-1970) by stating:

> I believe I have a good idea of the greatness of Christianity, but we are among those in this persecuted world who have the feeling that while Christ may have died for some people, he did not die for us. And at the same time, we refuse to let ourselves despair about man. Without having the unreasonable ambition of saving him, we try at least to serve him (Camus, *Essais*, 1965, 287).

Reflecting on Communism and Christianity in his *Notebooks*, he wrote: "The meaning of my works: so many men are deprived of mercy. How to live without mercy? One must try to do what Christianity never did: to take care of the damned" (Todd, 214). This idea of ministry to the damned is expressed even more forcefully in a letter he wrote to a Belgian divinity student:

> Tell yourself that three-quarters of the men in the Western world today are deprived of God and that one must try to formulate their thoughts consciously or not. Now is the time to do something for the damned . . . God has been and remains, I suppose, one of man's great opportunities. But all of those who have turned away from him must find another path, and must do so without too much pride or illusion (Todd, 215).

It is difficult to know whether Camus' comment in this letter that "God has been and remains, I suppose, one of man's great opportunities" is merely a token of courtesy to a young believer or a frank admission that theism might be right. What seems clear is that Camus found his own vocation in ministering "without too much pride or illusion" to people who had neither faith, nor certainty, nor hope of divine grace.

C. Plotinus, the Gnostics, and Saint Augustine

Twice in his life, Camus wrote philosophical studies that required intensive scholarship. The second of these studies, *The Rebel* (1956),

13

remains one of his better known books. The first, however, is relatively unknown. It is the thesis he submitted to The University Algiers in May of 1936 to earn a graduate diploma and apply for further study. Its title was *Christian Metaphysics and Neoplatonism* (*Métaphysique Chrétienne et Néoplatonisme*) and it ran about one hundred pages.

Since Camus was an enthusiastic Communist in 1936 as well as an atheist, his choice of Neoplatonism and Christian metaphysics as subjects for a thesis was rather odd. Jean Grenier, who was then teaching at the university, suggested Hindu philosophy, but Camus preferred a Christian focus. Part of the attraction may have been geographical. Both Plotinus and Saint Augustine were born in North Africa. As a French Algerian, Camus took pride in their North African origin and assumed that they shared with him a "Mediterranean" outlook. But Camus was also attracted to the deep interest that Plotinus, Augustine, and the Gnostics had in the problem of evil.

The problem of evil has two concerns: the evil that people do (moral evil) and the unjustified evil that sometimes happens to people (unjustified pain and suffering). These dual concerns can also be expressed through two common questions: Why do people do bad things? Why do bad things happen to good people?

In answer to the first question, it is often said that moral evil arises from the deficiencies of *individual* human beings—deficiencies such as inborn character flaws (e.g. tendencies to be mean or cowardly), or weakness of will, or bad habits, or ignorance. But some thinkers have argued that evil arises in large measure from deficiencies that are worldwide rather than individual—deficiencies in the world itself or in human nature. The great Greek philosopher Plato (427-348 BC) suggested something like this when he described the physical world as imprecise and ever-changing reflections of the perfect and unchangeable world of Forms. For Plato, those who rely on the physical world to teach them about the good are condemned to follow shadows. The Biblical story of Adam and Eve's "fall" in the Garden of Eden and the doctrine of original sin provide another way of connecting evil to worldwide conditions. The proposed connection is that physical and moral evils are common in the world because nature itself as well as human nature were corrupted by Adam and Eve's fall. In short, as heirs of Adam and Eve we are fallen creatures in a fallen world. Camus suggests that the problem of evil is at the center of Christianity.

In the three centuries after the death of Jesus, Christianity, Gnosticism, and Neoplatonism gained prominence in the Roman

14

Empire. Gnosticism constructed worldviews based in part on secret knowledge. The Greek word *'gnosis'* means 'knowledge.' Neoplatonists constructed worldviews based in part on the philosophy Plato had created centuries earlier. Although different in many respects, these worldviews shared a common concern with reconciling the perfection of a Supreme Being with the imperfections of the world. They sought to answer questions such as the following: Why did a perfect being create an imperfect world? Why does a perfect being permit its continuing existence? Why do people do bad things? Why do bad things happen to good people? By what means can a human being escape the imperfections of this world and become united with divine perfection? Of course, the answers they gave were not in agreement, but their intense and often ingenious debates produced an era of philosophical and theological vitality. It was this era that Camus chose to write about. His most general claim is that Greek and Christian thought evolved over three centuries of debate and eventually came together in the philosophy of Saint Augustine (354-430 AD).

Christian Metaphysics and Neoplatonism is the work of a talented graduate student who was more interested in grand themes than scholarly research. Since Camus had limited skills in reading Latin and practically none in Greek, he depended heavily on translations and secondary sources. Paul Archambault, a contemporary scholar of religious thought, has argued quite persuasively that Camus' interpretations are often careless and occasionally plagiarized. While Camus wrote the text, he was not above "reproducing—sometimes verbatim—ideas contained in his secondary sources, while referring the reader to the primary source, as if the discovery were his own" (Archambault, 50). Why did Camus permit himself these lapses in academic integrity? Part of the answer is that he was in a hurry to complete the requirements that would enable him to work as a philosophy professor. He probably never expected his thesis to be published, and the advisors who read it were not experts in this area. Yet despite its deficiencies, *Christian Metaphysics and Neoplatonism* provides useful insights into Camus' acquaintance with philosophers who wrestled with the challenge of reconciling an imperfect world with their belief in a perfect being. Of particular interest are Plotinus, St. Augustine, and three Christian Gnostics: Basilides, Marcion, and Valentinus.

15

1. Plotinus

Plotinus responded to the problem of evil in the world by blaming evil on "matter." The perfect One, from whom all being emanates, is the origin of everything that is good and nothing that is not good. But the degree of goodness at each level (hypostasis) of being depends on how close it is to the One. The physical world is the last and lowest level of being. It is farthest from the One. It is being at its thinnest. At this stage being is dispersed by a three-dimensional field of sheer indeterminacy that Plotinus identifies with matter. The effect of matter on being might be compared with effect of a shattered mirror on the faintest rays of light: it disperses the faintest emanations of being in many directions without absorbing that being. Matter for Plotinus is an absence (or privation) of being that produces the variety and disorder of the physical world.

However, Plotinus was not entirely consistent in his treatment of evil in the world. At times, he stressed the imperfection of bodily existence. According to Porphyry, his student and biographer, Plotinus seemed ashamed of being in a body and refused to have his portrait painted. At other times, Plotinus praised the beauty of the physical world. In *Christian Metaphysics and Neoplatonism*, Camus takes note of both tendencies. For example, he writes:

> To a certain extent Plotinus' Reason is already Pascal's "heart." . . . Plotinus' philosophy is an artist's point of view. If things are understandable it is because things are beautiful. But this extreme emotion that seizes the artist before the beauty of the world, Plotinus transports to the intelligible world. He admires the universe to the detriment of nature (Camus, *Essais*, 1965, 1271).

Why did a perfect being create an imperfect world? Why does He permit an imperfect world to exist? According to Plotinus, the process of divine creation was not a choice made in time, but an eternal overflowing (emanation) of being from the perfect One. If the being that flowed from the One had been perfect, it would have been the One itself and nothing new would have been created. But since all being is good and there was no jealousy in the One, a second level of being flowed from the One. That level was Intelligence (which includes Plato's Forms.) From Intelligence, there flowed a third stage of being:

16

Soul. Soul put life in the universe: divine, human, and animal. Soul is also responsible for bringing reflections of the Forms into the physical world.

By what means can a human being escape the imperfections of this world and become united with divine perfection? According to Plotinus, there is a returning "conversion" back to the One as well as a procession of being away from the One. Camus describes it this way:

> It is in the Soul that the principle of conversion is found. The Soul is desire for God and nostalgia for a lost homeland. Life without God is only a shadow of life. All beings strive toward God on the ladder of Ideas and tend to climb back up the course of procession. Only matter, this great pauper, this nothing-positive, does not aspire to God, and it is in it that the principle of evil resides (Camus, *Essais*, 1965, 1282).

For Plotinus, it is possible even in this life to achieve a temporary mystical union with the One, although permanent return must wait for the release of our souls from our bodies.

Why do bad things happen to good people? Plotinus is at his weakest in trying to explain the distribution of evil and suffering in the world. He asserts that evil exists only for wicked people. He affirms that there is an order in the universe that ultimately rewards or punishes people according to their merits. But he does not make a convincing case for either reward or punishment.

Although Camus borrowed relatively little from the details of Plotinus' philosophy, he was drawn to the idea that an all-embracing unity was necessary to explain the diversity of the material world. The discovery that the universe lacked such unity was sufficient to prove its absurdity. Camus was also fascinated with the general notion that to live in this world is to live in exile afflicted with "nostalgia for a lost homeland." In one of his earliest essays, "Summer in Algiers," he ponders the difficulty of staying focused on the present and the simple satisfactions of the tangible world. He asks: "Is there anything odd in finding on earth that union that Plotinus longed for? Unity is expressed here in terms of sun and sea" (Camus, *Myth*, 1955, 112). Over the years, and especially after Camus moved from Algeria to France, this notion of exile and nostalgia for a lost homeland became a central theme in his writings.

For example, it resonates with special intensity in his play, *The*

17

Misunderstanding. This play tells that story of a mother and daughter (Martha) who keep a small inn in an isolated village in Czechoslovakia. They have become so obsessed with saving enough money to leave their gloomy surroundings and move to a sunny home on the edge of a sea that they have made a practice of killing guests who occasionally find their way to the inn and stealing their money. One day a man arrives seeking a room. This man is the mother's son and Martha's brother, Jan. Yet they fail to recognize him. Jan left the village as a young man and made his fortune abroad, but he neglected to help or even write to his mother and sister. Now, he has returned to his homeland to surprise them and make amends for twenty years of neglect.

Curious to see how long it will take for them to recognize him, Jan gives a false name and pretends to be a stranger. But Jan's pretense proves disastrous. The mother and sister drug him and throw him into the river to die. Going through his things, they find his passport and discover his true identity. The mother is grief-stricken and throws herself into the river. Martha is horrified, not by Jan's death, but by her mother's abandonment of her and the crushing of her dream to live by the sea. When Jan's wife, Maria, comes to the inn looking for Jan, Martha tells her the truth and gives her some savage advice:

> MARTHA . . . But fix this is your mind, neither for him nor for us, neither in life nor in death is there any peace or homeland. . . . For you'll agree one can hardly call home, that place of clotted darkness underground, to which we go from here to feed blind animals.
>
> MARIA . . . It was to find another homeland that he crossed sea.
>
> MARTHA . . . We're cheated, I tell you. Cheated! What do they serve, those blind impulses that surge up in us, the yearning that rack our souls. Why cry out for sea, or for love? What futility! Your husband knows now what the answer is: that charnel house where in the end we shall all lie huddled side by side (Camus, *CTOP*, 1962, 132-133).

Like Martha, Camus thought that yearning for undisturbed peace in a lost homeland (Plotinus' dream) is futile, but, unlike her, he struggled to understand whether the way one lives one's life really matters.

2. The Gnostics

A more radical treatment of the problem of evil in the world was developed in the teaching of the Gnostics. The Gnostics were philosophers and religious teachers who achieved considerable influence in the early centuries of the Common Era (AD). The Gnostics were dualists who taught that being is divided into two realms: a divine realm of light that is good and a worldly realm of darkness that is evil. Human beings, they claimed, are trapped in the evil realm and require hidden knowledge (*gnosis*) in order to free the "inner man" and achieve salvation. Often this knowledge was cloaked in the language of mystical rites. Most of the Gnostics incorporated elements of Christianity into their teachings. But some borrowed doctrines from other religions, especially the Zoroastrian religion of ancient Persia.

In *Christian Metaphysics and Neoplatonism*, Camus focuses on Christian Gnosticism, which he describes as "one of the first attempts at Greco-Christian collaboration" (Camus, *Essais*, 1965, 1250). He claims that, despite differences among Gnostics, all of Gnosticism exhibits fundamental themes: "the problem of evil, redemption, the theory of intermediaries, and a conception of God as ineffable and incommunicable" (Camus, *Essais*, 1965, 1252). He then draws particular attention to three Christian Gnostics: Basilides, Marcion, and Valentinus.

He says of Basilides: "If it is true that the problem of evil is at the center of all Christian thought, then no one has been more profoundly Christian than Basilides" (Camus, *Essais*, 1965, 1252-1253). He attributes to Basilides three key thesis: 1) that human beings are naturally predisposed to sin; 2) that sin always leads to punishment; 3) that suffering is always tied to individual atonement and reform. The third thesis is especially interesting for it implies that the suffering of the Christian martyrs and even of Jesus Christ was suffered in atonement for their sins. "Even Christ," Camus remarks, "does not escape the universal law of sin" (Camus, *Essais*, 1965, 1254).

Marcion, as Camus points out, is notable for his view that there are two Gods: "the superior one reigns in the invisible world, the other, subordinate, is the God of this world" (Camus, *Essais*, 1965, 1255). Marcion identifies the second God with the God of the Old Testament and characterizes Him as a cruel and warlike deity. He is the God who persecuted Job to test the power of Satan, who called for blood and battles, who wrote the law that oppressed the Jewish people. The superior God is a hidden God, who was not revealed until Jesus made Him known. Although human beings are creatures of the lower world, they possess seeds of the superior God, and thus become a battleground in the struggle between the aggressive but inferior God of this world and the superior but very remote God of the invisible world. Indeed, the task of saving man is delegated to an intermediary:

> Jesus accomplishes here below a revolutionary mission. If he atones for our sins, it is that in so doing he combats the work of the cruel God. Emancipator as much as Redeemer, he is the instrument of a kind of metaphysical *coup d'état* (Camus, *Essais*, 1965, 1256).

Valentinus, a second generation Gnostic, defended a much more elaborate system of intermediaries, including groups of angels. Camus dubs this system "a Christian Olympus" (Camus, *Essais*, 1965, 1259). Valentinus described the process by which all this came about in terms that resembles the successive emanations of Plotinus. Valentinus' God like Plotinus' is solitary and perfect, a superabundance of being outside of time. The rest of being is the overflow from God's perfection. However, this process does not go smoothly. Sophia (wisdom) mismanages the generation of humanity just as another cosmic principle (the Demi-Urge) is creating the material world and the result is the formation of three distinct categories of human beings. Camus explains that these categories are determined by the degree to which one is conscious of one's origins:

> The spirituals who aspire to God, the materialists who neither know nor care about their origins, and between these two, the psychics, undecided, who wish for the crude life of the senses with the highest anxieties without knowing where to draw the line (Camus, *Essais*, 1965, 1260).

According to Camus, Valentinus' solution to the problem of evil is very simple. Because of Sophia's failure, the human soul lacks free will. The only people who will be saved are those who retain consciousness of their origins: the spirituals (or Gnostics). Although Camus does not point it out, there is a striking parallel between Valentinus' three categories of humans and Pascal's orders of flesh, mind, and charity. For Pascal, as for Valentinus, only those in the highest order have the knowledge needed to ensure salvation. In response to the question "Why did a perfect being create an imperfect world?" the Christian Gnostics are unanimous in saying that the perfect God did *not* create this world. The creator was an inferior being, a second-rate deity, who may be cruel and brutal as well. On the other hand, Christian Gnostics are neither unanimous nor very explicit on why a perfect being *permits* an imperfect world to exist. Perhaps the most that can be said in general is that the perfect being, the true God, is so remote from this world, so abstract, that any personal intervention would be unthinkable. The struggle with the realm of darkness must be conducted by intermediaries. "By what means can a human being escape the imperfections of this world and become united with divine perfection?" Here the Christian Gnostics are in agreement that *gnosis*, the hidden knowledge of God, is the key to salvation. "Why do bad things happen to good people?" The Gnostic answer is, "they don't." Humans are prone to sin, and suffering is punishment for sin. Bad things happen to bad people.

In Camus' later writings, Gnostic themes are reflected with particular intensity in his best play *Caligula*, a powerful short story called "The Renegade," and a dreary fantasy play entitled *State of Siege*.

In Camus' *Caligula*, the young emperor of Rome is impelled by the death Drusilla, his sister and lover, to seek a cure for the absurdity of a world in which "men die and are not happy" by reaching for the moon and by teaching his subjects what it means to live in an absurd world. As Paul Archambault has argued, *Caligula* can be read as a grotesque experiment in Gnosticism. The higher reality for which the young emperor longs, "the impossible," "the moon," "eternal life," can be identified with the realm of the superior God. He says at one point: "it's something higher, far above the gods, that I'm aiming at, longing for with my heart and soul" (Camus, *CTOP* 1962, 16). By the same token, Caligula's cruel and perverse reign can be seen as an enactment, a magnification of the essential darkness of this world. As for Caligula himself, he can be seen as a Gnostic teacher or even a would-be "intermediary," who takes up the task of bringing hidden knowledge to his subjects. "For I know what they need and haven't got. They're without understanding and they need a teacher; someone who knows

21

what he's talking about" (Camus, *CTOP* 1962, 9).

In a memorable scene, Caligula forces a group of patricians to worship him in a mystery ritual in which he stands on a pedestal dressed as the goddess Venus. But the Venus Caligula pretends to be is no goddess of love. The words of the ritual with which "she" is welcomed cast her in the role of Marcion's Gnostic deity of the lower world. "Bestow your gifts on us, and shed on our faces the light of your impartial cruelty, your wanton hatred; unfold above our eyes your arms laden with flowers and murders" (Camus, *CTOP* 1962, 42).

In Camus' *State of Siege*, Marcion's Gnostic deity of the lower world is represented by a character called The Plague. Although he first appears as a man who demands absolute authority over the city of Cadiz, he soon reveals that he is the personification of pestilence. Near the end of the play, as his power crumbles in the face of rebellion, he challenges the Judeo-Christian conception of God and justifies himself with a distinctly Gnostic argument:

> In the old days you professed to fear God and his caprices. But your God was an anarchist who played fast and loose with logic. He thought he could be autocratic and kindhearted at the same time—but that was wishful thinking, if I may put it so. *I*, anyhow, know better. I stand for power and power alone (Camus, *CTOP* 1962, 226).

Furthermore, The Plague finds hope for his eventual return to power in the conviction that most human beings lack the knowledge (*gnosis*), good will, and independence necessary for their redemption. He says:

> Those are your former masters returning, and you will find them blind as ever to the wounds of others, sodden with inertia and forgetfulness of the lessons of the past. And when you see stupidity getting the upper hand again without struggle, you will lose heart. . . . All honor, then, to the stupid, who prepare my ways (Camus, *CTOP* 1962, 227).

Of course, The Plague can also be seen as a personification of totalitarianism. He is the fascist, Nazi, or Communist dictator who rules by murder. In *State of Siege*, as in his novel *The Plague*, Camus uses pestilence as a symbol for political as well as natural and/or supernatural evil.

22

Camus' gripping short story "The Renegade" is the tale of a young missionary, a Protestant convert to Catholicism, who tries to Christianize a brutal tribe of idol-worshipers living in a city carved out of salt in an isolated corner of the North African desert. His dream of conquering the tribe by the power of the Word collapses immediately. He is imprisoned by guards in the dark, salt hut that contains their ax-faced idol—"the Fetish." In the stifling heat and stench of that hut he is stripped, oiled, and whipped across the face as a consecrated offering to the Fetish. He remains a prisoner in the hut and witnesses the daily ritual in which the tribe's Sorcerer rapes a woman kneeling on her hands and knees. One day the Sorcerer leaves a nearly naked woman in the hut, and the missionary has sexual intercourse with her. Then, for reasons we can only guess at (punishment, sacrifice, sanctification?), the priest and his assistant cut out the missionary's tongue. Blinded by pain and gagging on his own blood, the missionary prays for death, but death doesn't come.

Gradually he recovers from the wound. Speechless now in the misery of the hut, he renounces Christianity and surrenders his soul to the Fetish, whom he imagines to be the principle of hatred and cruelty. Like Basilides, he reasons that Christ must have deserved his punishment on the cross. Thus, the would-be missionary becomes a convert himself, a renegade from Christianity. Ironically, he never knows whether his beliefs about the Fetish correspond to the beliefs of the tribe. What is apparent is that this man cannot bear to live without devoting himself to one god or another. Desperate to find meaning in the world, he would rather worship an ax-faced idol of wrath and cruelty than face the absurdity of a meaningless world.

But the story does not end there. When French soldiers come to pacify the city of salt, the missionary-turned-renegade hopes that his captors will fight these outsiders with unrelenting ferocity. In fact, they do nothing of the kind. They bow to the superior might of the soldiers and agree to have their children instructed by a new Catholic missionary. The renegade, outraged by this betrayal, and intent on serving the Fetish, steals a rifle and shoots the new missionary. Again, he fails to complete his mission. The tribesmen, fearing retaliation by the soldiers, beat him viciously on a cross-shaped war saddle. "O Fetish," he cries, "why hast thou forsaken me?" (Camus, *EK*, 1991, 60). As dawn breaks on the desert, the renegade hears a voice (perhaps that of the wounded, new missionary) calling him back to Christianity. Addressing the Sorcerer, the renegade once again switches his faith:

"we'll begin all over again, we'll rebuild the city of mercy, I want to go back home" (Camus, *EK*, 1991, 61).

3. Saint Augustine

In *Christian Metaphysics and Neoplatonism*, Camus describes St. Augustine, the man, in terms that remind one of Camus himself:

> Deeply passionate, sensual, the fear of not being able to stay continent [abstain from sex] deferred his conversion for a long time. At the same time, he had a taste for rational truths. . . . But the problem of evil obsessed him. . . . And he was haunted by the idea of death (Camus, *Essais*, 1962, 1294-1295).

As for Augustine's worldview, Camus regards it as a culmination and synthesis of four centuries of intellectual struggle between Christianity and Greek philosophy. In opposition to Plotinus and the Gnostics, Augustine affirms the Judeo-Christian doctrine that God is both immanent (in the world) and transcendent (outside the world). God the creator and judge of this world is also God, the eternal redeemer and perfect being. Augustine's belief in God's perfections, especially his conviction that God is all-good, all-powerful, all-knowing, and present-everywhere provides him with a foundation for answering the questions posed above: Why did a perfect being create an imperfect world? Why does He permit an imperfect world to exist? Why do people do bad things? Why do bad things happen to good people? By what means can a human being escape the imperfections of this world and become united with divine perfection?

According to Augustine, God and all of the reality which He created are good. Indeed, the mere fact of existence is good. But the goodness of beings varies with their degree of perfection. Out of His own goodness, God created a vast gradation of beings—all good, but differing in their degrees of goodness. Augustine contends that nothing in nature is evil in-itself. Evil in nature, he says, is merely a name for the lack of good. The only positive evil is sin, and sin is something for which *we*, not God, are responsible. If things in nature appear evil to us, it is only because humankind lives under a sentence of death as just punishment for sin, and our frail bodies are vulnerable to the misuse of things around us. Fire, for example, is good in itself, although fire when misused can cause death and destruction. Even natural disasters such as plagues and famines only appear to be evil because we fail to see the roles they play in God's larger plan. It is God's glory to ensure that the imperfections of nature and even the sins of creatures with free will ultimately lead to good.

"Why do bad things happen to good people?" Augustine's answer is that there are no good people. (In Latin: *"nemo bonus."*) As a result of original sin, the human will is corrupted and human beings have lost the power to be good. In *Christian Metaphysics and Neoplatonism*, Camus explains this view in the following way:

> God left us the free will of Adam, but our will gained the desire to serve evil. And we are so profoundly perverted that it is only through God that free will can ever be properly used. Left to himself, man would possess only wickedness, deceit, and sin (Camus, *Essais,* 1965, 1297).

According to Augustine, Adam and Eve had the power to choose between good and evil. The descendants of Adam and Eve lack that power. It is futile for human beings to strive for virtue on their own or to seek to become worthy of salvation by performing good deeds. As Camus points out: "Saint Augustine insists on the vanity of virtue itself. Grace first, then virtue . . ." (Camus, *Essais,* 1965, 1297).

The concept of grace is fundamental to Augustine's worldview. He believes that God's grace is the only means by which human beings can rise above the imperfections of this world and their own sinful nature to dwell in God's heavenly city. But how can one obtain God's grace? Here, Augustine gives an answer that has provoked controversy among Christians for sixteen centuries. (It was, for example, at the heart of the Jansenist controversy, which preoccupied Pascal and his family.) Augustine says that God's grace is a free gift. Since no human being is capable of earning grace, it is an act of generosity on God's part to bestow grace on some members of the human race. Furthermore, God has known from all eternity which human beings He will elect to populate His heavenly city. Although Augustine insists that God does not cause our actions, he maintains that God knows precisely what we will do at every moment of our lives as well as what will happen to us after death. Thus, a person, like Augustine himself, who was inspired to give up sinful ways and seek salvation through faith and the sacraments of the Church may hope that he or she will turn out to be one of God's elect, but that person can never be sure what the future will bring.

Camus found Augustine's views on grace and salvation deeply disturbing. He was particularly offended by the idea that all human beings, even children, deserved damnation. In *Christian Metaphysics and Neoplatonism*, he writes:

> We depend on divine grace. Moreover, damnation is in principle universal. The entire human race is condemned to the flames. Its only hope is the mercy of God. From which follows another consequence: the damnation of unbaptized children (Camus, *Essais* 1965, 1301).

Actually, Augustine's position on the damnation of unbaptized children was not quite as harsh as Camus suggests. Augustine held that, although they were barred from salvation, their punishment would be the mildest possible. (In the thirteenth century, St. Thomas Aquinas assigned unbaptized children and virtuous pagans to eternal limbo—a place without the rewards of heaven *or* the torments of hell.) Nevertheless, Camus fastened onto Augustine's tough views on grace, especially the fate of unbaptized children, as emblematic of the harshness and elitism of Christianity. If God denies grace to most of humanity, then there is a desperate need to minister—without God's help—to the damned.

In his later work, Camus drew upon an Augustinian interpretation of Christianity in portraying Father Paneloux in *The Plague*. Indeed, Paneloux is introduced in this novel as a Jesuit who "had won a high place in his order" for research on "St. Augustine and the African Church" (Camus, *Plague* 1948, 84). Paneloux has been asked by his superiors to deliver a sermon on the recent outbreak of bubonic plague in the Algerian city Oran. The sermon he gives reflects his Augustinian confidence in the sinfulness of humanity and the unerring work of God's providence. He begins the sermon with the words: "Calamity has come on you, my brethren, and my brethren you deserved it" (Camus, *Plague* 1948, 84). He portrays the plague as an instrument of divine justice:

> For plague is the flail of God and the world his threshing floor, and implacably He will thresh out his harvest until the wheat

26

is separated from the chaff. There will be more chaff than wheat, few chosen of the many called (Camus, *Plague* 1948, 87).

Months later, after witnessing the agonizing death of a child infected with the plague, Paneloux gives another sermon. The second sermon is equally firm in its affirmation of God and but frankly skeptical about the human capacity to understand God's justice and providence. Paneloux still assumes that if we could see the whole tapestry that God's providence has woven, we would recognize that the world is not absurd, but he concedes that there are things in this world, such as the suffering of children, that surpass human comprehension. We shall return to Father Paneloux in Chapter 5.

Camus sometimes compared himself to St. Augustine *before* he found grace. In his last completed novel, *The Fall*, Camus creates a narrator who is a pure distillation of Augustinian guilt without Augustinian grace. Jean-Baptiste Clamence is an ex-lawyer from Pairs who holds court in a sleazy Amsterdam bar frequented by sailors, thieves, and pimps. There, he lies in wait for middle-class visitors *to* whom he can confess his many sins and *from* whom he can wring similar confessions. St. Augustine is famous for having created a landmark of Christian art and thought in his *Confessions*. Clamence also makes an art of confession, but his purpose is to diminish his own sense of guilt "by extending the condemnation to all, without distinction, in order to thin it out at the start" (Camus, *Fall*, 1991, 130).

Since Clamence is a self-confessed liar, it is difficult to know what he really believes. But like St. Augustine, he claims that no one is good: "[W] e cannot assert the innocence of anyone, whereas we can state with certainty the guilt of all" (Camus, *Fall*, 1991, 110). Clamence has created the role of judge-penitent (*juge-pénitent*) to surmount his own sins by using them as bait to lure other sinners into self-judgment. He accepts no excuses and offers no absolution. But he claims that the confessions of others make him feel "like God the Father" (Camus, *Fall* 1991, 143).

What is missing, of course, is the helping hand of a merciful God. At the end of *The Fall*, Clamence hints that the snow falling from the sky might be angelic messengers bringing news of mercy more generous than that envisioned by St. Augustine: "What an invasion! Let's hope they are bringing good news. Everyone will be saved, eh?—and not only the elect" (Camus, *Fall* 1991, 145). But these hints

27

remain playful and ambiguous. What we know with greater certainty is that Clamence can escape neither his relentless selfishness nor his incessant guilt over that selfishness. In Chapter 5, we will examine in greater detail the philosophical import of *The Fall*.

Pascal, Plotinus, Basilides, Marcion, Valentinus, and Augustine provided the religious roots out of which Camus' philosophical thought first emerged. Other religious thinkers, such as Dostoyevsky, Kierkegaard, Chestov, and Jaspers would help to shape the development of his thought in subsequent years.

What are we to make of Camus' enduring fascination with a religion he rejected? One plausible answer is suggested by Jean-Paul Sartre's remark to Camus: "there is a hatred of God which emerges in your books, to the point where one could call you 'anti-theist' still more than 'atheist' " (Sartre 1965, 99). For an atheist, God is irrelevant. Most atheists feel that faith in God should be swept into the same historical dustbin as fear of witches and goblins. For an "anti-theist," God is not irrelevant. An anti-theist holds that God's absence, or silence, or lack of mercy leaves a hole in the world that is too great to ignore. Like Sartre, Camus found no compelling reason to believe in God and even less reason to believe in an afterlife. But unlike Sartre, he was not certain that God did not exist. Camus admitted three possibilities and all three made him angry. Either there is no God and humankind is abandoned in a universe indifferent to human needs, or God is silent, or God speaks to and saves some people (the elect) but ignores the rest of humankind.

3
The Stranger

A. A Philosophical Reading of *The Stranger*

The opening sentences of *The Stranger* are among the most famous in twentieth century literature:

> "Maman died today. Or yesterday maybe, I don't know. I got a telegram from the home: 'Mother deceased. Funeral tomorrow. Faithfully yours.' That doesn't mean anything. Maybe it was yesterday" (Camus, *Stranger* 1988, 3).

What is so arresting about these spare sentences is that they deliver an immediate and disturbing impression of the stranger we are about to meet. The French word *'Maman'* is a word that a child would use to refer to his mother. It is similar to the English words 'Mama' or 'Mom.' Thus, the first sentence is personal in tone. It suggests that the speaker was close to his *Maman* and is saddened by her loss. But the second sentence suggests something very different. It shifts attention from the sadness of death to the date of death. The remaining sentences confirm this impression. The speaker sounds more like a clerk checking on date of death than a son mourning for his mother. The inclusion of the telegram from the old people's home points—

almost mockingly—at the telegraphic style of the speaker: short disconnected sentences. Telegrams were written in as few words as possible because one had to pay by the word. The speaker of this novel is nearly as stingy with his words. As Sartre observed in his 1943 review of *The Stranger*, the sentences of this novel are "islands" (Sartre *LE* 1957, 24).

Who is the speaker of *The Stranger*? As the novel unfolds, we discover that the speaker is a young bachelor who lives in Algiers and holds an office job with a small company. We find out that his last name is Meursault, yet we never discover his first name or much about his past. We learn that he never knew his father and that he shared his apartment with his mother until three years before her death. He mentions that he lost his ambitions when he had to give up his studies, although this explanation seems insufficient to explain his lack of interest in his own future. He says that he had lived in Paris at one time. Other than these few details, the years before his mother's death remain a blank for us.

The novel is divided into two roughly equal parts. Part One has six chapters; Part Two has five chapters. Part One covers a period of eleven days; it begins with Meursault's discovery that his mother has died and ends with his killing an Arab on the beach. Part Two covers a period of eleven months; it begins with Meursault's interrogation by the examining magistrate and ends with Meursault's reflections on the absurd as he waits in his cell to learn whether his sentence of death will be commuted.

In Part One, we see the mundane rhythms of Meursault's life. He eats, he sleeps, he smokes, he works at the office. On his days off, he goes to the beach or sits on his balcony and watches people pass by on the street below. He doesn't talk much, and when he does talk he is usually bluntly honest about what he is thinking. In this respect, Meursault is like the character Alceste in Moliere's play *The Misanthrope*. But Alceste chooses to be bluntly honest as a matter of principle, while Meursault does it spontaneously. Meursault tells people what he is really thinking not because he wishes to challenge or offend them, but because he cannot be bothered to do otherwise. Even when it would be to his advantage to lie or avoid telling the whole truth, he does not conceal his beliefs.

Meursault seldom thinks of the past or the future. He lives each day as it comes, and what matters most to him in the course of a day are the sensory pleasures or discomforts that his circumstances afford. He is particularly sensitive to the North African sun: enjoying its clear light and warmth at times; oppressed by its scorching heat at other times. He is also sensitive to his girlfriend Marie. He appreciates her pretty smile, tan skin, and nice figure. He pays attention to how she looks and expresses his appreciation. He says, for example: "She had put on a white linen dress and let her hair down. I told her she was beautiful, and she laughed with delight" (Camus *Stranger* 1989, 47). But Meursault also pays attention to physical details that most people would overlook or regard as trivial. At work, for instance, he enjoys drying his hands at midday when the towel in the bathroom is dry, but he is irritated by its sogginess at the end of the day.

Meursault lives in a French working-class neighborhood of Algiers, like the Belcourt neighborhood in which Camus grew up. His friends and neighbors have little money or education. Marie is a secretary; Céleste keeps a neighborhood café; Emmanuel is a dispatcher; Salamano is a retiree who lives alone with his dog; Raymond claims to work at a warehouse but is reputed to be a pimp. As Gerald Kamber demonstrated in "The Allegory of the Names in *L'Etranger*," the names of these characters suggest an array of subtly complementary meanings. Marie, for example, bears the same name as the Virgin Mary. Céleste, whose name means "celestial," is a fat, down-to-earth cook who exemplifies human kindness. Emmanuel, who is close to being a simpleton, has a name that was used to describe Christ. His name in Hebrew means "God is with us."

Despite the ordinariness of Meursault and his friends, the principal events of Part One are far from ordinary. In the space of eleven days, Meursault does all of the following. He attends his mother's funeral. He begins an affair with Marie and agrees to marry her. He becomes friends with Raymond and agrees to help Raymond punish his former mistress for cheating on him. He shoots and kills the brother of Raymond's mistress. For a mundane man, these are eventful days.

On the other hand, the way in which Meursault becomes involved in these events exhibits a characteristic pattern of passivity. In each case, the event arises by chance rather than by premeditation, and Meursault responds by taking what feels to him like the path of least resistance. His mother dies, and he reluctantly attends her funeral. He meets Marie by chance at the beach, swims with her, invites her to a movie and takes her back to his apartment, where they spend the night together. Meursault's sexual interest in Marie is not passive; he finds her attractive and desirable. But when Marie stops by a week later and suddenly asks Meursault whether he wants to marry her, his response is astonishingly passive.

> I said it didn't make any difference to me and that we could if she wanted to. Then she wanted to know if I loved her. I answered the same way I had the last time, that it didn't mean anything but that I probably didn't love her. "So why marry me, then?" she said. I explained to her that it didn't really matter and that if she wanted to, we could get married. Besides she was the one who was doing the asking and all I was saying was yes. Then she pointed out that marriage was a serious thing. I said, "No." . . . She just wanted to know if I would have accepted the same proposal from another woman, with whom I was involved in the same way. I said, "Sure" (Camus, *Stranger*, 1989, 41-42).

Meursault also bumps into Raymond by chance. Raymond invites him to his room to save him the trouble of cooking. After dinner, Raymond asks him to write a letter to his former mistress, whom he has already beaten "till she bled," in order to lure her back so that he could punish her again. Meursault accepts. "I wrote the letter. I did it just as it came to me, but I tried my best to please Raymond because I didn't have any reason not to please him" (Camus *Stranger*, 1988, 41-42).

Meursault's encounter on the beach with the brother of Raymond's former mistress, is also a matter of chance. Although Meursault returns to the spot on the beach where he last saw the two Arabs, he is surprised to find anyone there. "As far as I was concerned the whole thing was over, and I'd gone there without even thinking about it" (Camus, *Stranger*, 1989, 58). But one of the Arabs is still there. (It is noteworthy that Meursault's victim, the brother of Raymond's former mistress, is referred to simply as "the Arab" ("*l'Arabe*"). Whether Camus did this to show the insensitivity of French Algerians or out of his own insensitivity, the effect is to reduce an individual to anonymity.) When "the Arab" puts his hand on the knife in his pants pocket, Meursault puts *his* hand on the pistol in his jacket pocket. From that point on, Meursault yields (as he sees it) to the fury of the sun. Overcome by the sun's blinding heat and light, he steps closer to the Arab, and the Arab draws his knife. The reflection of the sun from the blade strikes Meursault's face. Blinded and confused, Meursault squeezes the gun in his hand. The shot strikes the Arab. Meursault pauses and then fires four more times at the motionless body.

It is this last action—the firing of the four additional shots—that is hardest to explain. Unlike the first shot, which might have been an accident (a reflex or slip of the hand), the four subsequent shots were intentional acts. Why did Meursault pause and then pull the trigger four times when he could have chosen not to? What were his motives? What was his purpose? Despite the importance of these questions during his interrogation and trial, Meursault is unable to give a plausible explanation. It is clear that he fired the additional shots without knowing or even considering whether the Arab was alive or dead. Yet we have no reason to think that a strong emotion like hatred, anger, or fear, led to his action. Although his shooting showed callous disregard for the life of a man who had done him no wrong, it does not appear that he desired the death of this man. During the earlier encounter with the Arabs on the beach, it occurred to Meursault that "one could shoot or not shoot" (Camus, *TRN*, 1962, 1164). His last four shots seem to be fired out of inertia rather than out of initiative.

In Part Two of *The Stranger*, the chance events and Meursault's passive responses in Part One are linked together by the officials of the criminal justice system in Algiers to portray Meursault as a monster. The process begins in earnest with Meursault's interrogation by the prosecuting attorney (*le juge d'instruction*) When Meursault is unable to explain why he paused after the first shot and then fired four more bullets into the Arab's body, the prosecutor takes out a silver crucifix and waves it in Meursault's face. He asks Meursault whether he believes in God. When Meursault says "no," he becomes indignant.

> He said it was impossible; all men believe in God, even those who turn their backs on him. That was his belief, and if he were ever to doubt it, his life would become meaningless. "Do you want my life to be meaningless?" he shouted (Camus, *Stranger*, 1989, 69).

By the end of this interrogation the prosecuting attorney is referring to Meursault as "Mr. Antichrist" ("*Monsieur l'Antéchrist*"). The point of attaching this absurd label to Meursault is to make his hard-to-explain behavior understandable to respectable Christians. If one assumes that Meursault is the incarnation of evil, then all of his actions in Part One can be explained in the same way.

The process begun by the prosecuting attorney is carried forward at the trial by the court prosecutor (*"le procureur"*). The prosecutor dwells at great length on Meursault's behavior at his mother's funeral, accusing him at one point of "burying his mother with crime in his heart" and finally of being "morally guilty of killing his mother" (Camus, *Stranger* 1989, 96, 101-102). He links together Meursault's affair with Marie and the letter for Raymond with his "motive" for killing the Arab:

> The same man who the day after his mother died was indulging in the most shameful debauchery killed a man for the most trivial of reasons and did so in order to settle an affair of unspeakable vice" (Camus, *Stranger* 1989, 96, 101-102).

In his summation at the end of the trial, the prosecutor goes even further. Excited by his own rhetoric, he attempts to connect Meursault's "guilt" with the upcoming trial of a man accused of murdering his father:

> [A] man who is morally guilty of killing his mother severs himself from society in the same way as the man who raises a murderous hand against the father who begat him. In any case, the one man paved the way for the deeds of the other, in a sense foreshadowed and even legitimized them. "I am convinced, gentlemen," he added, raising his voice, "that you will not think it too bold of me if I suggest to you that the man who is seated in the dock is also guilty of the murder to be tried tomorrow (Camus, *Stranger* 1989, 102).

The prosecutor says that it is his "painful duty" to call for the death penalty, but notes that this duty is "made easier, lighter, clearer, by the certain knowledge of a sacred imperative and by the horror I feel when I look into a man's face and all I see is a monster (*que de monstrueux*) (Camus, *Stranger* 1989, 102, *TRN*, 1962, 1198). The jury obliges, and Meursault is sentenced to be guillotined in a public square.

What are we to make of Meursault's trial? As a young reporter for *Alger Républicain*, Camus often covered criminal trials in Algiers and knew first-hand the frailties of the system. He even took the liberty of giving himself a cameo appearance in *The Stranger*. Early in the trial, Meursault notices that the youngest reporter in the room, a man wearing gray flannel pants and a blue tie, is staring at him. "All I could see in his slightly lop-sided face were his two very bright eyes staring at me . . . And I had the odd impression of being watched by myself." (Camus, *Stranger* 1989, 85). No doubt, Camus intended Meursault's trial to serve in part as a commentary on the criminal justice system. He knew from experience how lawyers could twist evidence to make a case. He knew how they could invoke God, mother, and country for their own purposes. He knew how self-righteous and lethal judges and juries could be.

Yet there is also a philosophical side to this trial. The grotesque accusations of the prosecuting attorney and the court prosecutor may make a mockery of criminal justice, but they are not without purpose. Meursault represents a real threat. Although he is certainly neither a hardened criminal nor the Antichrist, he is an incarnation of the absurd hero. What is "monstrous" about this man is not his propensity to commit crimes or do evil; it is, rather, his indifference to the hopes, faith, and ideals by which most people live. By not caring about God, his own future, or what respectable people think about him, Meursault has become a dangerous man, a rebel. To be sure, he has broken a man-made law against homicide, but that infraction is secondary to his outspoken indifference toward the religious and moral order of the universe. It is bad enough that Meursault does not share their beliefs; it is infuriating that he will not pretend to share their beliefs. The prosecuting attorney puts his finger on this danger when he responds to Meursault's denial of belief in God by shouting: "Do you want my life to be meaningless?" (Camus, *Stranger*, 1989, 69). While those who judge Meursault may not fully comprehend that the threat he poses is philosophical rather than criminal, they sense the danger he represents.

Of course, it is true that Meursault has killed a man without an intelligible motive for doing so and without expressing remorse for the life he has taken. One could imagine a different trial in which Meursault was committed to a hospital for the criminally insane because of worries about his capacity to distinguish right from wrong and the unpredictability of his conduct. But that is not the trial that takes place. An unstated premise of the trial that does take place is the racism in Algeria under French rule. Because Meursault is a white European and his victim an Arab, there is a presumption that Meursault will be given favorable treatment. This may help explain why Meursault's lawyer seems confident at first that things will go well. But Meursault forfeits this advantage by refusing to acknowledge the common bonds of Christianity, feign grief over his mother's death, or express remorse for killing the Arab. He has shown himself to be "a stranger," *"un étranger,"* which in French can mean a foreigner or outsider as well as a person you do not know. As such, he is severed from the ruling society that could have protected him. His condemnation to the guillotine is given a kind of racial legitimacy by the prosecutor's insistence that he is "morally guilty" of killing his own mother and the father of the (presumably white) man on trial for parricide.

After his trial, Meursault is moved to another cell, a death row cell, to await execution. He has made an appeal for clemency, but he has no idea whether that appeal will be granted. He spends his days and nights dreaming about a loophole in the execution process and waiting to learn whether he will be reprieved or taken off to the guillotine.

Although Meursault has repeatedly refused to see the prison chaplain, the chaplain comes to his cell anyway. At first Meursault shudders, since he thinks the hour of his execution has arrived. The chaplain reassures him that that is not the case and expresses confidence that the appeal will be granted. The purpose of his visit, he explains, is to turn Meursault's attention from human justice to divine justice, from legal guilt to mortal sin. Meursault replies that he does not believe in God and has no interest in wasting the little time that may be left to him worrying about an afterlife. When the chaplain promises Meursault that, despite his blind heart, he will pray for him, Meursault cracks. Instead of evading confrontation by pretending to agree or ceasing to listen, as Meursault usually does, he grabs the priest by his cassock and begins shouting and insulting him. He tells the priest "that none of his certainties [is] worth a hair from a woman's head" and he could not even know whether he was alive "because he was living like a dead man" (Camus, *TRN* 1962, 1208). Guards enter the cell and release the chaplain from Meursault's grasp.

Exhausted by his confrontation, Meursault falls asleep on his bunk. When he awakens "stars are on [his] face" (Camus *Stranger* 1989, 122). A breeze is blowing into his cell with smells of night, earth, and salt air. Once again, Meursault is revitalized by contact with the physical world. His words, normally so prosaic, become lyrical. "Then in the dark before dawn sirens blasted. They were announcing departures for a world that now and forever meant nothing to me" (Camus *Stranger* 1989, 122). For the first time in many weeks, he thinks of his "Maman" and recalls the romance she began with old Thomas Pérez, her "fiancé" at the home. Meursault recognizes that, he, too, is ready to relive his life.

> As if that great anger had purged me of every ill, emptied me
> of hope; for the first time, in that night alive with signs and
> stars, I opened my heart to the gentle indifference of the
> world. Finding it so much like myself—so fraternal really—I
> felt that I had been happy and that I was happy again (Camus,
> *TRN*, 1962, 1209).

Eager to live but reconciled with death, he hopes that there will be
many spectators on the day of his execution and that they will greet him
"with cries of hate" (Camus, *Stranger*, 1989, 123).

C. A Philosophical Critique of *The Stranger*

For philosophical purposes, the most important chapter in *The
Stranger* is the final chapter of the book. It is in this chapter that
Meursault first finds the words to express his convictions about the
inescapable absurdity of human life. Interestingly, those words are
prompted by the efforts of the prison chaplain. This priest notes, as
Pascal had done, that everyone is condemned to death, and that sooner
or later each of us will have to face the issues of God's judgment and
eternal destiny. Meursault tells the chaplain that he does not believe in
God or an afterlife and that he does not want to waste whatever time he
has left thinking about subjects that he is certain do not interest him.
When the priest insists that Meursault describe the kind of afterlife he
would *wish for*, Meursault shouts: "One where I could remember this
life!" (Camus, *Stranger*, 1989, 120). Meursault's love of earthly life,
even in the face of death, is deeply distressing to the chaplain. As a
traditional Roman Catholic priest, he regards earthly life as a vale of
tears in a fallen world where true and lasting happiness is not possible.
He presses Meursault, and Meursault explodes.

The words that Camus selects to describe Meursault's outburst are
revealing. "I poured out on him everything that was at the bottom of
my heart with surges mixed of anger and joy" (Camus, *TRN* 1962,
1208). Meursault is not just abusing the priest; he is disclosing for the
first time what is truly in his heart. In a sense, this confrontation is also
a confession. By putting into words his deepest convictions about the

essential absurdity of life, Meursault denies the need for divine forgiveness and absolves himself of any misgivings about the ultimate significance of the choices he has made.

What is the essential absurdity of life? Meursault attempts to explain in it in the passage that follows. For the sake of philosophical emphasis, I have translated the French verb *'importer'* as 'to have importance' rather than the more natural 'to matter.'

> I had lived my life in one way and I could have lived it in another way. I had done this and I had not done that. . . . Nothing, nothing had importance, and I knew why. So did he. From the far end of my future, throughout this absurd life [*vie absurde*] I had been leading, a dark wind had been blowing against me . . . What importance could they have for me, the deaths of others, a mother's love? What importance could his God have, or the lives people choose, the destinies they elect, since one destiny alone must elect me, and with me billions of privileged people who, like him, called themselves my brothers? . . . The others would all be condemned one day. And he, too, would be condemned (Camus, *TRN* 1962, 1208-1209).

The meaning of this passage is critical for a philosophical critique of *The Stranger*, since it is the only place in the novel where Meursault, the speaker and main character, attempts to give a philosophical explanation for his beliefs about the human condition. Yet the explanation presented in this passage seems incomplete in several respects. Let us examine what is missing in this formulation and try to determine how it should or could be completed.

At the most basic level, Meursault is saying that the lives people lead and the choices they make lack "importance" because sooner or later everybody dies. What is not stated in this passage is that death is the end of a human being's existence as a person or conscious being. If there were an afterlife, a heaven and hell for example, then what a person did in this life might very well have importance for the next life. But Meursault has already denied any belief in a divinity or an afterlife, and this denial serves as an unstated premise for his explanation. Meursault's denial of the divine also rules out a Stoic interpretation. The Greek and Roman Stoics urged "apathy" towards life's fortunes and misfortunes, but they based this advice on their conviction that all events are governed providentially by divine reason.

Another unstated premise is supplied by Meursault's unflagging affirmation of life itself. At no point in this novel is there any indication that Meursault is tired of living or contemplating suicide. On the contrary, he is a man who savors each day and the simplest pleasures afforded by his physical surroundings. Even his life in prison becomes tolerable after a while, and he imagines that he could get used to living in the trunk of a hollow tree. At the very end of the novel, he says that he has had a happy life and that he is still happy. Clearly then, life itself is not unimportant to Meursault. Indeed, it is possible that he thinks of life as having intrinsic value for all human beings.

What is it that *lacks* importance? The "examples" Meursault mentions suggest that the answer may be the *particular* choices, actions, and events that make up the lives of different individuals.

> What importance would it have if, accused of murder, he was executed for not crying at his mother's funeral? Salamano's dog was worth as much as his wife. . . . What importance did it have that Raymond was as much my pal as Céleste who was worth more than him? What importance did it have that Marie today gave her lips to a new Meursault? (Camus, *TRN,* 1962, 1209).

With these examples in mind, Meursault's assertion that "nothing had importance" could be taken to mean "although life itself is important, the way one lives and the choices one makes are not important. This is consistent with Meursault's remark to his boss in Part I: "one life is as good as another" (Camus, *Stranger,* 1989, 40).

Yet this is not the whole story. What remains to be understood is the kind of "importance" that Meursault is speaking of here. The word 'importance,' whether in French or English, is generally used as an implicitly relational term. To say that 'x has importance' is to suggest that 'x has importance *for* or *to* y.' Furthermore, x can be important to y as a *means,* an *end,* or both. Throughout much of life, Camus searched for a permanent cure to his own tuberculosis. A cure for tuberculosis had importance *for* Camus as a *means to* serve the *end* of a longer and healthier life.

How, then, should we understand Meursault's claim that our particular lives and choices have no importance because sooner or later everyone dies? If what he means by "importance" is short for "importance for an afterlife" and we grant his assumption that there is no afterlife, then his claim is logically valid but tautological (i.e. true by assumption or definition). On the other hand, an individual's choices and the results of those choices are usually important to that person in the sense that he or she cares about them as means or ends. Moreover, some of those choices are likely to have importance for other people when that individual is dead.

Even Meursault is far from indifferent to the physical stimuli of his surroundings. According to his own testimony, he shoots the Arab because he is overcome by the stifling heat of the sun. He was revived after his confrontation with the chaplain by "smells of the night, earth and salt air cooling his temples" (Camus, *Stranger*, 1989, 122). When he complained to his boss about the soggy towel in the washroom at the end, his boss shrugged it off as "a detail without importance" (Camus, *TRN*, 1962, 1141-1142), but clearly it had some importance for Meursault.

Moreover, Meursault attaches some importance to the attitudes that other people display toward him. When Céleste looks at him apologetically "with trembling lips," after his earnest but ineffective testimony in court, Meursault says, "it was the first time in my life I ever wanted to kiss a man" (Camus, *Stranger*, 1989, 93). We cannot know what importance, if any, Meursault's life and choices might have on other people after his death, but it is easy to imagine that they might have importance for Marie or Raymond, or even the chaplain whose "eyes were full of tears" after his confrontation with Meursault (Camus, *Stranger*, 1989, 122).

If the view that "the way one lives and the choices one makes lack *importance* because of death's finality" is to escape being tautological or false, then 'importance' here must mean something broader than 'importance for an afterlife' and narrower than 'importance of any kind.' But what could that be? A good candidate for this interpretation is 'importance beyond the interests of individual human beings.' What this interpretation excludes is any kind of moral order or hierarchy of values which depends on something other than the interests (i.e. needs, desires, preferences, wishes etc.) of individual human beings. Under this interpretation, human choices and actions derive no importance from gods, fates, eternal values, natural rights, or the laws of history. Thus, Meursault's view can be understood to mean: "Because of death's finality, the way one lives and the choices one makes lack importance beyond the interests of individual human beings."

40

What remains to be clarified is whether Meursault thinks that life itself has the same kind of importance as particular choices and actions, or whether he thinks that it has some kind of intrinsic or universal importance. It may be, as Meursault told his boss, that one life is as good as another, but how good is life itself? Meursault clearly attaches importance to his own life, he enjoys being alive. But is this importance just one more manifestation of individual desire or does it reflect something universal? Is life as an end-in-itself for all humans? And if it is, why do tens of thousands of people every year commit suicide? Are there grounds for believing that every human being *ought* to value life itself? The text of *The Stranger* suggests these questions, but it does not provide answers. For Camus' reflections on the importance of life itself, one must turn to *The Myth of Sisyphus*, which opens with the pronouncement: "There is but one truly serious philosophical problem, and that is suicide (Camus, *Myth*, 1955, 3).

Meursault's reflections at the end of *The Stranger* also prompt but leave open two questions about the concern of individuals for other people. The first is the question of selfishness. To what extent, if any, *do* individuals act so as to serve other people's interests as ends-in-themselves, and not merely as a means for serving their own interests? The second is the question of moral obligation to others? To what extent, if any, *ought* individuals to act so as to serve other people's interests as ends-in-themselves, and not merely as a means for serving their own interests?

For now, let us note that these questions are connected in an interesting way to Meursault's reflections on death and the absurdity of life. If, as he assumes, there is no afterlife or external moral order *and* an individual is indifferent to the interests of other people, then it is easy to see why death will strip his life of all importance. It is not merely that he won't care what happens *after* he is dead. It is also that during his life he will not attach importance to any future state in which his own interests will not be affected. If, on the other hand, the interests of other people are important to him as ends-in-themselves, then he will attach importance to future states after his death which will affect the lives of people he cares about. Consider two examples. Most parents sacrifice for the future of their children and attach importance to the quality of lives that their children will lead after they are gone. Many environmentalists work hard to protect the environment because they believe they ought to share the Earth's resources with future generations and attach importance to the quality of lives they will never

41

know.

This attitude is foreign to Meursault. We have no reason to think that he is concerned about what will happen to other people after he is dead. He is not totally indifferent to the needs and desires of other people. But his capacity for sympathy is feebler than that of most people and he does not believe that he *ought* to be concerned about other people's interests. He likes to please people whose company he enjoys, but he loses interest in people who are not part of his physical environment. He seldom thought about his mother after she moved to the old people's home, and he loses interest in Marie during his months in prison. Just before the chaplain's visit, he says:

> For the first time in a long time I thought about Marie. The days had been long since she stopped writing. That evening I thought about it and told myself that maybe she had gotten tired of being the girlfriend of a condemned man. It also occurred to me that maybe she was sick or dead. These things happen. How was I to know, since apart from our bodies together there wasn't anything to remind us of each other? Anyway, after that remembering Marie meant nothing to me. (Camus, *Stranger* 1989, 115).

Compared to most people, Meursault's feelings of sympathy and moral concern for others are noticeably deficient. Yet he possesses an enviable capacity for enjoying the very texture of life itself. In "Summer in Algiers" Camus remarks: "It requires a rare vocation to be a sensualist" (Camus, *Myth* 1955, 113). Meursault has that rare vocation. He says that if he had "to live in the trunk of a dead tree, with nothing to do but look up at the sky flowering overhead . . . [he] would have gotten used to it" (Camus, *The Stranger* 1989, 77). In this, Meursault is a vivid exception to Pascal's portrait of man without God. He *is* content to stay quietly in his own chamber—even if that chamber were the trunk of a tree. He does not yearn for travel, adventure, or other diversions. When he finally "thinks closely" on "our feeble and mortal condition," he finds it a cause for happiness rather than a source of inconsolable misery. It is this exceptional outlook that enables him to achieve conscious harmony with "the gentle indifference of the world" at the end of the novel (Camus, *Stranger*, 1989, 122).

The last paragraph of *The Stranger* is one of the most moving passages in all of twentieth century literature. But the simple poetry of this paragraph belies its complexity. Let us take a close look at the several strands that make up this passage.

> I felt as if I understood why at the end of her life she had taken a fiancé and why she had played at beginning again. . . . So close to death, Maman must have felt free then and ready to relive everything (à *tout revivre*). Nobody, nobody had the right to cry over her. And I too felt ready to relive everything (à *tout revivre*). (Camus, *TRN*, 1962, 1209).

What these lines suggest is not merely an appreciation for life in the face of death, but the notion that death can free us "to relive everything." It seems likely that what Camus had in mind in choosing this expression was Nietzsche's theory of eternal recurrence. While still in high school, Camus had had begun reading the vivid, unsystematic works of Friedrich Wilhelm Nietzsche, a German philosopher of astonishing originality. In some of his writings Nietzsche entertained the hypothesis that the universe was a finite sum of energy with a very large but finite number of possible states (or combinations). He reasoned that eventually the entire sequence of possible states would be exhausted and the universe would repeat itself. This would happen not once but an infinite number of times. Whether Nietzsche intended this as a serious cosmological theory is questionable, but he found it useful as a test for the affirmation of life and self. In *The Gay Science*, for example, he asks you to imagine how you would react if a demon appeared in your loneliest moment and revealed that every detail of your life would be repeated innumerable times in precisely the same order. Would this revelation crush you? Or would it fill you with joy? Most people, Nietzsche thought, would be crushed by this revelation. Only those rare individuals who had regrets neither about life itself nor about how they had lived their lives would rejoice over this revelation.

Nevertheless, Meursault's success in living without regrets has a foundation that is quite different from the foundation that Nietzsche envisioned. (Alexander Nehamas' *Nietzsche: Life as Literature* provides an outstanding interpretation of Nietzsche's views on this issue.) For Nietzsche, the proper foundation is strength of will attained through the coordination of one's impulses. It is self-mastery and the creation of a unified self. But Meursault can hardly be said to master or create himself. Meursault just comes to know himself. His confrontation/confession with the chaplain has enabled him to see with clarity that what is important to him is earthly life at the level of sensuous awareness. Unlike most people, the indifference of the world to human quests for meaning and hope does not matter to him. He has no yearning for cosmic unity and intelligibility, no need to connect his present to past and future. He finds the world to be like himself, and that makes him happy. "I opened my heart to the gentle indifference of the world. Finding it so much like myself—so fraternal really—I felt that I had been happy and that I was happy again" (Camus, *TRN* 1962, 1209).

But the novel's final sentence strikes a new and discordant note:

> For everything to be consummated, and for me to feel less alone, it only remained for me to wish that there would be many spectators on the day of my execution and that they would greet me with cries of hate" (Camus, *TRN*, 1989, 1209-1210).

What are we to make of this? In *The Myth of Sisyphus*, Camus stresses the importance of scorn as a source of strength for the absurd man in the face adversity. We are told that even the crushing burden of Sisyphus' rock can be overcome through the power of scorn. "There is no fate," says Camus, "that cannot be surmounted by scorn" (Camus, *Myth*, 1955, 90). In *The Stranger*, however, this idea does not appear until the end of the novel, and we do not see it in action. Meursault too lives the absurd, but his success in living without false hope or illusion derives from not caring rather than overcoming. He is rather like Franz Kafka's character in "The Hunger Artist" who can fast for as long as he chooses—even to death—because he could never find a food that he liked. The hunger artist creates a vocation and way of life based on his lack of interest in food, but this is not a lack that most of us share. Meursault is an absurd man and, by virtue of his relentless honesty, something of an absurd hero, but he is too much of an aberration to serve as a model for others. Nevertheless, this mundane clerk constitutes one of Camus' most remarkable experiments in presenting an absurd worldview through the life of an individual. In the other works of his absurdist trilogy, Camus experiments with more grandiose figures: a Roman emperor and a mythical trickster king.

4
CALIGULA AND SISYPHUS

A. Caligula

Camus' play *Caligula* takes as its subject a real person: Gaius Julius Caesar Germanicus, nicknamed Caligula ("little boots"), who ruled from 37-41 AD as the fourth Emperor of the Roman Empire. The real emperor, like Camus' character, quickly lost interest in expanding the empire and concentrated his attention on life in Rome. After an illness early in his reign, his conduct became increasingly cruel and bizarre. He was the first Roman emperor to abandon the trappings of republican government and the first to declare himself a living god. He enjoyed the company of actors and gladiators and sometimes appeared in the arena himself. According to the Roman historian Suetonius (75-150 AD), he suffered from acute insomnia, liked to wear women's clothing, and indulged in every form of debauchery—including incest with his three sisters. He was despised by Roman patricians (aristocrats) and reviled by Christians and Jews. Some Christians believed he was the Antichrist. Finally, a group of senators persuaded Cassius Chaerea, an officer in the praetorian (palace) guard, to assassinate Caligula. On January 24, 41 AD, Caligula and his fourth wife Caesonia were stabbed to death in a corridor underneath the palace.   Another praetorian guard grabbed their baby daughter and dashed out her brains against the wall.

Nearly every detail of Camus' *Caligula* is based on Suetonius' account of Caligula in *Twelve Caesars*. Yet Camus reworks these details to tell a story that makes no pretense at being historically accurate. This is a drama of ideas, not a dramatizing of history. The play begins shortly after the death of Drusilla, Caligula's sister and lover. The shock of this loss sends Caligula wandering through the Roman countryside and crystallizes his recognition of the absurd. After returning to the palace, he formulates this recognition as "a simple, obvious, almost silly truth . . . Men die; and they are not happy" (Camus, *CTOP*, 1962, 8).

We do not see Caligula before Drusilla's death, but we are told that he was dependable, humane, and rather conventional.   Caesonia, presented here as his faithful mistress, describes the "old" Caligula in these terms. "He told me life isn't easy, but it has consolations: religion, art, and the love one inspires in others. He often told me that the only mistake one makes in life is to cause sufferings" (Camus, *CTOP*, 1958, 10). The "new" Caligula is not dependable, humane, or conventional. He has undergone a kind of *irreligious* conversion. He has become an apostle and an enforcer of the absurd truth that "men die and are not happy."

What Caligula means by "men die" is essentially the same as what Meursault meant when he said that nothing has importance because one destiny (death) chooses everyone. But his assertion that human beings are not happy expresses a new idea.   Taken literally and without qualification, this assertion seems to be false or exaggerated. After all, most human beings are happy sometimes and unhappy at other times. A more plausible—although less dramatic—interpretation of Caligula's assertion is that human happiness is fragile and temporary. This is also Pascal's point of departure. Despite all our efforts to make ourselves happy, we often fall short of the mark. Sometimes we do not get what we work for. Sometimes we get what we want and find ourselves disappointed.   When we are successful, our success is temporary. Envy, boredom, or just plain restlessness can undermine happiness. Illness or financial distress can create misery. Even the luckiest people grow old, get sick sometimes, lose loved ones, and die.

Caligula describes the absurdity of the human condition with the phrase "men die and they are not happy," but he describes his own outlook in more subtle terms. Speaking of the death of his sister,

Drusilla, he says: "Most people imagine that a man suffers because out of the blue death snatches away the woman he loves. But his real suffering is less futile; it comes from the discovery that death, too, cannot last. Even grief is a vanity" (Camus, *CTOP*, 1962, 71). Caligula not only recognizes the fragility of human happiness, he also recognizes that most people are very adept and persistent at deceiving themselves about this fragility. He decides to liberate people from their illusions, and because he is the emperor he has the power to do it. He tells his friend Helicon:

> I'm surrounded by lies and self-deception. But I've had enough of that; I wish men to live by the light of truth. And I have the power to make them do so. For I know what they need and haven't got. They're without understanding and they need a teacher; someone who knows what he's talking about. (Camus, *CTOP*, 1962, 9).

Caligula fulfills his role as teacher by instituting a reign of terror in which his subjects, especially the patricians are arbitrarily abused, humiliated, cuckolded, and murdered. He sends wives of patricians to work in the public brothel. He creates a social order without justice and consistency in which every citizen lives in fear of summary execution. He reduces all of his subject to a single "privileged class"— condemned prisoners awaiting execution. The cruel absurdity of this social order is intended to be a mirror of the world's absurdity.

What is more difficult to determine is the connection between Caligula's reign of terror and his avowed goal to "reduce the sum of human suffering and make an end of death (Camus, *CTOP*, 1962, 16). It may be true that he reduces the normal Roman death rate by refusing to embark on wars. As he tells young Scipio, "even the smallest war . . . would cost you a thousand times more lives than all my vagaries . . . put together" (Camus *CTOP*, 1962, 44). Yet he increases the suffering of the people around him and does nothing to "make an end of death." Perhaps, the only way to make complete sense out of his goal is to follow Paul Archambault in interpreting Caligula's quest in Gnostic terms. If we assume that Caligula sees himself as an "intermediary" sent by the superior deity of the invisible world to take control of this world from evil gods, then his lofty goal does make sense.

A Gnostic interpretation would also allow us to make help us to understand the following exchange.

CAESONIA: But that's sheer madness, sheer madness. It's wanting to be a god on earth.

CALIGULA: So you, too, think I'm mad. And yet—what is a god that I should not wish to be his equal? No, it's something higher, far above the gods, that I'm aiming at, longing for with all my heart and soul. I am taking over a kingdom where the impossible is king.

. . . .

CAESONIA: [*facing him with an imploring gesture*]: There's good and bad, high and low, justice and injustice. And I swear to you these things will never change.

CALIGULA: [*in the same tone*]: And I'm resolved to change them . . . I shall give this age of ours a kingly gift—the gift of equality. And when all is leveled out, when the impossible has come to earth, and the moon is in my hands—then, perhaps, I shall be transfigured and the world renewed; then men will die no more and at last be happy (Camus, *CTOP* 1962, 16-17).

If we take Caligula's words literally, then we must assume that he is speaking of the salvation of the world and his own transfiguration through supernatural intervention. Like Christ, this Antichrist promises to triumph over death, renew the world, and end the guilt and suffering of humankind. If, however, we do not take Caligula's words literally, then a very different interpretation becomes possible. If we suppose that he is speaking of "moral and psychological" rather than "physical and metaphysical" transfiguration, renewal, and triumph over death, then supernatural help is not necessary. I believe a plausible interpretation of what Caligula is trying to accomplish on the plane of moral and psychological renewal can be given in terms of Nietzsche's philosophy. For example, Caligula's resolution to level out "good and bad, high and low, justice and injustice" bears a close resemblance to Nietzsche's summons at the beginning of *Beyond Good and Evil* to question "faith in opposite values":

For all the value that the true, the truthful, and the selfless may deserve, it would still be possible that a higher and more fundamental value for life might have to be ascribed to deception, selfishness, and lust. It might even be possible that what constitutes the value of these good and revealed things is precisely that they are insidiously related, tied to, and involved with these wicked, seemingly opposite things—maybe even one with them in essence. Maybe! (Nietzsche 1989, 10).

Unlike Meursault, Caligula does not find humankind's "feeble and mortal condition" a cause for happiness. Realizing that "men die and are not happy," he is profoundly disturbed and wants to do something about it. Part of what he does can be seen as a Nietzschean project of gaining mastery over himself. Shedding the yoke of traditional morality, he seeks the lonely freedom of self-creation. In *Twilight of the Idols*, Nietzsche demanded that the philosopher "take his stand *beyond* good and evil and leave the illusion of moral judgment *beneath* him" (Nietzsche 1954, 501). This is what Caligula does.

Unfortunately, Caligula is a philosopher with imperial powers, and he does not hesitate to impose his moral experiments on the people of Rome. Although he cannot overcome death, he can take control of how and when people die. Although he cannot guarantee happiness, he can become the dispenser of unhappiness. Caligula seeks to free himself from every bond of feeling, sentiment, and moral obligation. In a final act of liberation through cruelty he strangles his faithful mistress Caesonia and tells her: "I live, I kill, I exercise the rapturous power of a destroyer, compared with which the power of a creator is merest child's play. And this, *this* is happiness" (Camus, *CTOP*, 1962, 72).

The only character in the play who is neither terrified nor beguiled by Caligula is Cherea. Cherea admits to Caligula that he wishes to kill him because he is a menace to human security and happiness. He grants that Caligula's rule is a logical extension of his absurdist philosophy, but objects to a ruler who "is converting his philosophy into corpses" (Camus, *CTOP*, 1962, 21). Cherea insists that he is "an ordinary sort of man," a man who wishes "to live and be happy," (Camus, *CTOP*, 1962, 51-52). He finds it intolerable that Caligula is draining life of meaning. He holds to the basic principle that "some actions . . . are more praiseworthy than others" (Camus, *CTOP*, 1962, 72). It is Cherea who leads the frightened conspirators in assassinating Caligula, and it is Caligula who lets him do it. Indeed, Caligula, who has tortured and murdered his subjects for the most whimsical reasons, restores Cherea's "innocence" by destroying the wax tablet that incriminates him in the conspiracy.

A few moments before the conspirators arrive, Caligula confesses to his mirror that he has chosen the wrong path. Gazing at his own image, he screams: "I stretch out my hands but it's always you that I find, you only, confronting me, and I've come to hate you. I have chosen a wrong path a path that leads to nothing. My freedom isn't the right one . . . " (Camus, *CTOP*, 1962, 73).
Few people, I think, would disagree with this conclusion. Caligula's quest for the impossible has succeeded neither in Gnostic nor in Nietzschean terms. Superficially, he has shown his subjects how absurd life can be, but his "teaching" has not made a lasting difference. His subjects will, no doubt, return to their illusions as soon as he is dead. What remains in doubt, however, is the moral import of his declaration that he has "chosen the wrong path," that his "freedom isn't the right one" (Camus, *CTOP*, 1962, 72). Is Camus telling us that exercising "the rapturous powers of a destroyer" did not work for Caligula or is he telling us that it is morally wrong for any person to behave like this? If his message is the latter, he does not explain it. It remains to be seen whether Caligula's "path" can be shown to be morally wrong in some objective sense.
As Caligula dies from his wounds, he shrieks: "I am still alive!" (Camus, *CTOP*, 1962, 72). Critics have puzzled over the meaning of this closing line. I suspect Camus included it because Suetonius claimed that these were Caligula's last words and because they are dramatic words on which to end a play.

B. *The Myth of Sisyphus*

The Myth of Sisyphus is an essay in four parts that was first published in occupied France near the end of 1942. The parts are entitled: "An Absurd Reasoning," "The Absurd Man," "Absurd Creation," and "The Myth of Sisyphus." Camus' publisher, Gallimard, cut nearly fourteen pages from the book because they dealt with Franz Kafka (1883-1924). Kafka was a Jew and the German authorities in occupied France wanted to prevent favorable attention to Jewish authors. Curiously, the long passages on the philosophers Edmund Husserl and Leo Chestov were not cut, even though Chestov and Husserl were also Jewish. After the liberation of France, the pages on Kafka were restored as an appendix. The American edition of *The Myth of Sisyphus* also included two essays that Camus wrote in the 1930's and three that he wrote in 1950's.

The opening lines of The *Myth of Sisyphus*, the first paragraph of "An Absurd Reasoning," display both Camus' power as an essayist as and his casual attitude toward philosophical argument. He writes:

> There is but one truly philosophical problem, and that is suicide. Judging whether life is or is not worth living amounts to answering the fundamental question of philosophy. All the rest—whether or not the world has three dimensions, whether the mind has nine or twelve categories—comes afterwards (Camus, *Myth*, 1955, 3).

To be sure, judging whether life is worth living is a truly serious philosophical problem. But it is not the *only* truly serious philosophical problem, and it may not be the *first* problem that one ought to consider. The examples Camus gives of other philosophical problems, physical dimensions and categories of mind, are not fair examples. They are specialized issues not basic philosophical problems. On the other hand, a problem such as "What are the limits of human knowledge?" are is serious and, perhaps, prior to Camus' question, for it may help us to determine whether we can ever *know* whether life is worth living.

Camus proposes a test to decide whether one problem in philosophy is more urgent than another. His test is the "actions it entails." He writes:

> I see many people die because they judge that life is not worth living. I see others paradoxically getting killed for ideas or illusions that give them a reason for living (what is called a reason for living is also an excellent reason for dying) (Camus, *Myth*, 1955, 3).

This is a clever remark, but philosophically muddled. As Camus himself admits later on, "there are many causes for suicide" and only rarely do we find suicides that are committed "through reflection" (Camus, *Myth*, 1955, 3-4). Sometimes people commit suicide because they feel that their particular lives are not worth living and see no way to change their lives. Sometimes people commit suicide because they are clinically depressed and unable to think clearly about what matters to them. Few people commit suicide because they judge intellectually

51

that life itself is not worth living. Few people choose to die in defense of their reasons for living. Premeditated martyrs are very rare. Yet some people do put themselves at risk on behalf of their ideals, and occasionally lose their lives in the process.

Despite Camus' opening declaration, the problem with which "An Absurd Reasoning" actually deals is narrower and less dramatic than suicide in general. It is the problem of whether the conviction that life has no meaning commits one to the conclusion that life itself is not worth living. Or to put it another way: should a person convinced that life is absurd conclude that there is no point in continuing to live? To deal with this problem, Camus needs to clarify what is meant by saying "life has no meaning" or "life is absurd." He takes up this task in section two; a section called "Absurd Walls."

In "Absurd Walls," Camus stresses that the absurd arises from the "confrontation between human need and the unreasonable silence of the world" (Camus, *Myth*, 1955, 21). He argues that human beings are naturally disposed to want and expect the world to be intelligible in the full and familiar ways that religious and philosophical systems have portrayed it. (Meursault is clearly an exception.) This kind of intelligibility has two essential features. First, it purports to be comprehensive, to explain the world as a whole and not just a part of the world. As Camus insists: " I want everything to be explained to me or nothing" (Camus, *Myth*, 1955, 20). Second, it is intelligible in terms that human beings care about; it makes sense with respect to human values. He says: "The mind's deepest desire . . . is an insistence upon familiarity . . . . Understanding the world for a man is reducing it to the human, stamping it with his seal" (Camus, *Myth*, 1955, 13).

According to Camus, the absurd arises because the world lacks this kind of intelligibility. Although it is natural to speak about the absurdity of life or the absurdity of the world, neither expression is strictly correct. In the fullest sense, the absurd is the clear recognition that our longing for a world that can be fully understood in human terms is not satisfied by the world. We want the world to make sense, but it does not make sense. To see this conflict is to see the absurd.

> In this unintelligible and limited universe, man's fate henceforth assumes its meaning. . . . I said the world is absurd, but I was too hasty. . . . What is absurd is the confrontation of this irrational and the wild longing for clarity whose call echoes in the human heart. (Camus, *Myth*, 1955, 16).

The arguments that Camus uses to show that the world lacks this kind of intelligibility are sketchy at best. The finality of death, which served as the key argument in *The Stranger*, is mentioned but not given special priority in *The Myth of Sisyphus*. He also refers briefly to Sartre's early theory of Nausea as a revelation of the world's absurdity. But for the most part, he merely alludes to positions and arguments that other thinkers have developed. In particular, he refers to the writings of Nietzsche, Dostoyevsky, Kierkegaard, Kafka, Chestov, Heidegger, and Jaspers to reinforce his case for the unintelligibility of the world. He is content to illustrate rather than prove the unintelligibility of the world, for what really interests him are the consequences of this conviction. "I am interested—let me repeat again—not so much in absurd discoveries as in their consequences" (Camus, *Myth*, 1955, 12).

Nevertheless, Camus mentions in passing three general arguments for believing that the world is unintelligible. Let us examine each. First, he says, "after so many centuries of inquiries, so many abdications among thinkers . . . people despair of true knowledge" (Camus, *Myth*, 1955, 14). What Camus may have in mind here is the failure of philosophers to reach agreement on the solution of any basic philosophical problem by philosophical means. One way to explain this failure is by supposing that the world is unintelligible, but this is not the only way. Alternatively, one could suppose that the obstacle is not the world but the inadequacy of philosophy or some limitation of the human mind. In any case, there is no reason to suppose that system-making philosophy will be more successful in the future than it has been in the past.

Second, he claims that there are just two things of which I can say, "I know that!" (Camus, *Myth*, 1955, 14). One is my existence as a conscious being and the other is the existence of the world I can touch. "There ends my knowledge, and the rest is construction" (Camus, *Myth*, 1955, 14). Camus' claim here seems to be that one's own existence as consciousness and the existence of the tangible world are more immediate and harder to doubt than anything else. They are "givens," whereas other beliefs require assumptions and interpretations. As modest as this claim is, it has been challenged by some philosophers. Yet, even if this claim is right, it still does not follow that the world is unintelligible. What follows is that any "familiar" understanding we could have of the world as a whole will be less immediate and more provisional than the knowledge we have of our own existence as consciousness and the tangible world's existence.

Third, Camus dismisses natural science as a means of discovering the intelligibility of the world on the grounds that natural science ultimately relies on poetry, metaphor, or art. He gives only one specific example, atomic theory.

> At the final stage you teach me that this wondrous and multicolored universe can be reduced to the atom . . . . But you tell me of an invisible planetary system in which electrons gravitate around a nucleus. You explain this world to me with an image. I realize then that you have been reduced to poetry. . . . So that science that was to teach me everything ends up in hypothesis, that lucidity founders in metaphor, that uncertainty is resolved in a work of art (Camus, *Myth*, 1955, 15).

Although Camus compresses several different ideas about science in this passage, at least one idea is mistaken. Even in the 1930s, the analogy of the atom with a planetary system was not intended as an explanation of how atoms actually work. The image of an atom as a planetary system was and is an educational device for helping people— especially nonscientists—envision a theoretical account that can only be expressed with precision in mathematical terms. Camus seems to conflate the provisional and approximate status of scientific knowledge with the idea that science ultimately depends on poetry or art. Scientific knowledge is always provisional, but scientific theories need not depend on artistic images, metaphors, or analogies.

I believe the above arguments show that Camus is overly pessimistic about the scientific intelligibility of the world. Like Nietzsche and the contemporary American philosopher Richard Rorty, he is too quick to put all constructed knowledge on the same plane. He is too ready to dismiss the cautious, incomplete, and provisional convergence of empirical science on an understanding of the world as no more revealing about the way things really are than religious myths or philosophical speculation. He is too insistent that the intelligibility of the world must meet his demands for comprehensiveness and familiarity. On the other hand, I believe Camus is right in asserting that the world does not exhibit the kind of comforting unity, coherence, and relevance for human destiny that most human beings have wanted and expected. The world does seem indifferent to our individual and collective fates, and that is the kind of meaning most people crave.

Thomas Nagel, a contemporary American philosopher, has argued that Camus' account of the absurd is fundamentally mistaken. According to Nagel, "the absurdity of our situation derives not from a collision between our expectations and the world, but from a collision within ourselves" (Nagel, 17). This collision within ourselves arises from each person's capacity to take an external view of his or her own life in all its frantic particularity, while remaining thoroughly engaged in that life. Nagel thinks Camus' account of the absurd in terms of a collision between our expectations and the world fails because our situation could still be seen as absurd even if there were a larger meaning or purpose to the world. He argues:

> If we can step back from the purposes of individual life and doubt their point, we can step back from the progress of human history, or of science, of the success of a society, or the kingdom, power, and glory of God, and put these things in to question in the same way (Nagel, 16-17).

Yet Nagel's argument does not prove that Camus is wrong. At most, it illustrates that the absurd can have more than one interpretation. The human capacity to call into doubt any justification that might be given for a belief or value gives rise to one kind of absurdity—a rather abstract and philosophical kind of absurdity. On the other hand, Camus' "discovery" that the only meanings relevant to human destiny are those which human beings construct for themselves gives rise to a different kind of absurdity—a sense of cosmic homelessness. This contrast can best be understood by using Camus' favorite touchstone: Christianity. If Christianity is true, then each of my choices has meaning, value, and consequences that does not depend on personal preferences or social constructions. My existence, both in its mortal phase and in its eternal aftermath, is part of God's plan for the universe as whole. Of course, I can always ask: "What justification does God have for planning things this way?" But raising this question does not change the fact that God's plan invests my life with transcendent meaning about which I am probably not capable of being indifferent.

If Camus is right in asserting that the world lacks the kind of meaning or intelligibility we care about, why have so few people recognized this lack? I believe Camus' implicit answer is that people are skillful and persistent at deceiving themselves about the true nature of the world. Traditional religions, like Christianity, and philosophical

55

ideologies, like Marxism, are the myths that assist us in this process.
However, the myths of religion and philosophy are symptoms
rather than causes of the disposition to be deceived. Such myths are
grand illusions for shielding one's eyes from the absurd. On a more
mundane level, people acquire habits of thought and action which
produce a humbler refuge from the absurd. They surround themselves
with a stage set of familiar, constructed meanings. At the same time,
they cultivate the art of not thinking too deeply, the art of diverting
themselves from the graver aspects of the human condition. People
become so busy playing their daily roles as spouses, parents, friends,
jobholders, etc. that they fail to see the absurd. Most people live and
die without confronting the unintelligibility of the world. But
occasionally the illusion melts and one's defenses breakdown. Camus
puts it this way:

> It happens that the stage set collapses. Rising, streetcar, four
> hours in the office or factory, meal, streetcar, four hours of
> work, meal, sleep, and Monday, Tuesday, Wednesday,
> Thursday, Friday, Saturday according to the same rhythm—
> this path is easily followed most of the time. But one day the
> "why" arises and everything begins in that weariness tinged
> with amazement. (Camus, *Myth*, 1955, 10).

For Camus, the discovery of the absurd is liberating. It frees us
from our precious illusions. But the price of this freedom is high. If
the world has no moral order, no meaning, direction, or standards by
which our choices can be judged, how can we lead meaningful lives?
Camus thinks that few people are able to meet the challenge of
living in the face of the irrational, the absurd, without resorting to
evasion or self-deception. An attitude of unflinching honesty toward
the absurd requires "a total absence of hope . . . complete rejection . . .
and a conscious dissatisfaction" (Camus, *Myth*, 1955, 23). Even
philosophers who have achieved a firm intellectual grasp of the absurd
may choose to trample reason and embrace the unintelligibility of the
world as a cause for hope. Although Camus has yet to answer his own
key question about whether life is worth living in a meaningless world,
he turns now to consider two ways of evading the grip of that question.
The third section of "An Absurd Reasoning" is called
"Philosophical Suicide." In this section, Camus criticizes two
philosophical movements that were influential on the European

continent in the first half of the twentieth century. First, he criticizes the efforts of "existential philosophies" to escape the absurd through a religious leap of faith. Second, he criticizes the efforts of phenomenology to discover the essential laws of conscious experience. The common purpose of both critiques is to show that there is no honest way around the unintelligibility of the world.

Since the term 'existentialism' did not come into general use as a term for both religious and atheistic existentialists until after World War II, it is not surprising that Camus reserves this label for religious existentialists. Although *The Myth of Sisyphus* mentions Nietzsche, Heidegger, and Sartre, none is identified as an existentialist. The three thinkers that Camus does critique as examples of "existential thought" are Søren Kierkegaard, Lev Chestov (usually written in English as Leon Shestov) (1866-1938) and Karl Jaspers (1883-1969). Kierkegaard was a Dane who gave up his plans to become a Lutheran pastor in order to devote himself to writing unconventional books from a religious point of view. Chestov was a Russian who moved to France about the time Stalin came to power. His writing brought together Judaism and existential themes. Karl Jaspers was a German philosopher and psychologist who played a key role in the formulation of twentieth century existentialism. Unfortunately, what Camus has to say about these provocative thinkers is rather vague. While he seems to have read French translations of Chestov's *Potestas Clavium* (*The Power of the Keys*), Kierkegaard's essay *The Sickness unto Death* and parts of *The Journals of Søren Kierkegaard*, it is difficult to gauge the depth of his familiarity with the individual works and ideas of these thinkers.

What Camus does understand, however, is that Kierkegaard, Chestov, and Jaspers agree that the world cannot be comprehended by reason and yet find in this unintelligibility a cause for hope in a higher power. Unlike most advocates for Judaism and Christianity, they do not claim that the world becomes intelligible once we bring God into the picture. They do not think that the world offers clear evidence of God's plan for humankind. What these thinkers find in the world are reasons for doubt, dread, and despair. Yet, as Camus points out, "they deify what crushes them and find reason to hope in what impoverishes them" (Camus, *Myth*, 1955, 24).

The basic strategies for religious existentialists were pioneered by Kierkegaard in the middle of the nineteenth century, and he, in turn, was guided by a long tradition of Judeo-Christian fideism. Fideism is the view that faith in God does not need the support of reason or evidence. For Kierkegaard, religious faith is a matter of passion and will. The harder it is to believe in God, the heavier the need for passion and will, then the greater the faith achieved. Kierkegaard places Christianity above other religions not because it is more intelligible than other religions, but because it is more paradoxical. In his eyes, it is the "absolute difficulty" of being a Christian that gives it pride of place. Chestov and Jaspers follow Kierkegaard in finding hope in "a leap of faith" that goes beyond reason and measures the strength of that hope by the difficulty of the leap.

For Camus, these strategies are a kind of "philosophical suicide" (Camus, *Myth*, 1955, 31). Since reason reveals the unintelligibility of the world and the futility of hope, these existential thinkers kill reason in a desperate attempt to save hope. But Camus will have none of this. In his eyes, philosophical suicide is cowardly and self-deceptive. Better to live without hope in what theists call "sin and despair."

Camus' critique of Husserl's phenomenology has a different thrust. Husserl began his a career as a mathematician and was drawn to philosophy in order to gain a better understanding of the foundations of mathematics. By 1911, Husserl thought of phenomenology as a rigorous descriptive science for examining whatever appears, insofar as it appears and only insofar as it appears. By "bracketing off" the unsolvable problem of what exists outside of consciousness, he believed phenomenology could discover descriptive laws of consciousness as rigorous as the laws of theoretical science. For over fifty years, phenomenology thrived—with mixed success—as a new way of dealing with issues in philosophy and psychology. Among its practitioners were phenomenologists who followed Husserl in "bracketing off" existence (or being), and others, like Heidegger, Sartre, and Maurice Merleau-Ponty who used phenomenological methods to try to reveal the nature of being.

Camus challenges phenomenology in *The Myth of Sisyphus* for the same reason that he challenges the natural sciences. He wants to deflect any attempt to render the world as a whole intelligible. Camus begins by questioning Husserl's principle of intentionality. Husserl claimed that consciousness always "intends" or aims at an object. For example, whenever we hear a sound we hear it as a sound of something. I may be uncertain whether the cry I hear now is the cry of a child, an animal or TV set, but I experience that cry as the cry *of* something. Camus is willing to admit that intentionality might be a psychological feature of consciousness, but he objects strongly to

Husserl's linking of intentionality with essences. Husserl tried to show that phenomenology could reveal "essences," that are essential structures and necessary truths of consciousness. Camus simply dismisses these essences as another way of trying to restore the world to the rule of eternal reason and likens Husserl to Plotinus.

The final section of "An Absurd Reasoning" is called "Absurd Freedom." In this section, Camus returns from "philosophical suicide" to "plain suicide" (Camus, *Myth*, 1955, 37). Does the meaningless of the world imply that life is not worth living? Should a person convinced that life is absurd conclude that there is no point in continuing to live? Camus' answer is "no" and the key to this answer is his concept of "rebellion" (*"la révolte"*). Although Camus' exposition of this critical point is somewhat fuzzy, I believe it can be explained in the following way. According to Camus, people who think that their lives are worth living because of meaning they believe or hope is *in the world* are subordinating the worth of their lives to something external. Thus, people who think that life is worth living because God promises them a heavenly reward, or because they are serving the cause of history, or for some other *external* reason are treating their lives as means to ends rather than as ends-in-themselves. For Camus, to live life in its fullest majesty is to live it for its own sake in unflinching recognition of the absurd. Instead of being humbled by the world's unintelligibility and lack of hope, we should defiantly assert our independence by refusing hope and affirming life.

Camus calls rebellion "the first consequence" of the absurd and proceeds to argue for two additional consequences: freedom and passion (Camus, *Myth*, 1955, 41, 47). By "freedom" (*"la liberté"*), he means living the experience of liberation from everything outside of attention to life itself. To help make this understandable, he compares absurd freedom to the freedom of the slave, the mystic, and the condemned man. These are odd comparisons, but Camus is looking for ways to convey a sense of what it is like *not* to feel responsible for the world around us. He points, for example, to the condemned man's "unbelievable disinterestedness with regard to everything except for the pure flame of life" (Camus, *Myth*, 1955, 44).

Surprisingly, Camus denies that free will is relevant to his concerns. "Knowing whether or not man is free doesn't interest me. . . The problem of 'freedom as such' has no meaning" (Camus, *Myth*, 1955, 41). Although his reasons for dismissing free will are far from clear, he seems to think that free will must be bound up in some way

59

with God, eternity, or an order of reality beyond the observable world.

The third consequence of the absurd is passion. By "passion," Camus means constant consciousness "of the present and succession of presents" (Camus, *Myth*, 1955, 47). To live to the maximum is to be "aware of one's life, one's revolt, and to the maximum" (Camus, *Myth*, 1955, 46). This consequence returns us to the question raised in the previous chapter: Are there grounds for believing that every human being *ought* to value life itself? Camus answer is "yes," although his reasons for saying "yes" are rather fuzzy. What Camus seems to believe is that our conscious experience of living in the world is a good-in-itself for human beings. Moreover, he seems to be in agreement with Thomas Nagel's inference:

> Therefore life is worth living even when the bad elements of experience are plentiful, and the good ones too meager to outweigh the bad ones are their own. The additional positive weight is supplied by experience itself, rather than by any of its contents (Nagel, 2).

Camus stresses the desirability of maximizing this good-in-itself by learning to seize the day and savor the flow of experience.

Camus adds that for those who do this, the critical difference among lives is length. "Thus it is that no depth, no emotion, no passion, and no sacrifice could render equal in the eyes of the absurd man (even if he wished so) a conscious life of forty years and a lucidity spread over sixty years" (Camus, *Myth*, 1955, 46-47). This is a striking claim and rather poignant, since Camus' tuberculosis made him worry about a premature death. Yet as an unqualified generalization, this claim is not very convincing. Although people who prize life for its own sake prefer to live longer than shorter lives, few, I think, would agree with Camus that quantity is always more important than quality. Compare, for example, forty years spent doing what one enjoys in the company of good friends and family with sixty years spent alone in a prison cell. Perhaps someone as strange as Meursault would choose the latter over the former, but even that is doubtful given his enjoyment of sun, sand, and sea, his fondness for the company of people without pretensions, and his willingness to accept death when it comes.

Camus concludes "An Absurd Reasoning" with a decisive answer to his opening question. Rather than leading to suicide, the discovery of the absurd leads—according to this reasoning—to a defiant, liberating, and passionate affirmation of life. Camus admits that this is not all that one needs to know about life. "But," he declares, "the point is to live" (Camus, *Myth*, 1955, 48).

How good is Camus' argument in "An Absurd Reasoning"? In terms of reasoning, it is spotty at best. I have already noted some of the places where this argument falters in point of clarity, fact, or logic. There are other places as well. But spotty arguments need not lead to false conclusions. How good are Camus' conclusions? To help answer this question, let us take a moment to consider the last part of *The Myth of the Sisyphus*, the part which bears the title "The Myth of Sisyphus."

In "The Myth of Sisyphus," Camus takes the trickster king Sisyphus from Greco-Roman mythology and transforms him into an absurd hero. Camus' Sisyphus is a man who loves life and the beauty of earth. After his death, he implores Pluto to let him return to the upper-world to punish his wife. Pluto agrees, but once Sisyphus rediscovers the joy of "water and sun, warm stones and the sea," he refuses to go back to the land of the dead. Finally, Mercury is sent to drag him back—this time to be punished forever. Sisyphus's punishment is to spend eternity pushing a huge rock to the top of a mountain, from where the rock rolls back down of its own weight. The gods "thought with some reason that there is no more dreadful punishment than futile and hopeless labor" (Camus, *Myth*, 1955, 88).

What does Sisyphus think about as he walks back down the mountain? The ancient sources do not tell us, but Camus breathes into Sisyphus an afterlife of passionate lucidity and everlasting revolt. That Sisyphus is conscious of his fate stands to reason, for "where would his torture be, if at every step the hope of succeeding upheld him?" (Camus, *Myth*, 1955, 89-90). Sisyphus sees with perfect lucidity the meaninglessness of his labor and the tragedy of his condition. He knows that his future will be indistinguishable from his present. All that he can change is the attitude with which he confronts his fate. The gods have assumed that Sisyphus will be crushed by the misery of his fate. But Sisyphus in Camus' tale proves stronger than the gods. He scorns the gods by embracing his labor with perverse enthusiasm and by refusing to be miserable. "There is no fate," says Camus, "that cannot be surmounted by scorn" (Camus, *Myth*, 1955, 90).

Camus goes further. He suggests that Sisyphus is able to find happiness (*le bonheur*) by defiantly recapturing his fate. There are two ingredients here: one is revolt and the other is ownership. To the extent that one can live without appeal to any hope or help that a deity might provide, one becomes one's own master and in that mastery lies a pure form of happiness. "Happiness and the absurd are sons of the same earth" (Camus, *Myth*, 1955, 90). The recognition that "all is well" drives out of this world "a god who came into it ... with a preference for futile suffering" and makes of fate "a human matter, which must be settled among men" (Camus, *Myth*, 1955, 91). "The struggle itself toward the heights is enough to fill a man's heart. One must imagine Sisyphus happy" (Camus, *Myth*, 1955, 91).

These are beautifully crafted and stirring lines, but do they contain useful lessons? Can lucidity, revolt, liberation, and passion, as Camus has described them, produce self-mastery and happiness? It is certainly possible to think of extreme situations where these ingredients might be the best recipe for people who want to maintain a grip on life and self without turning to religion. In a recent article on *The Myth of Sisyphus*, James Wood cites the example of Primo Levi at Auschwitz. Levi, a non-believer, confessed in *The Drowned and the Damned*, that there was one moment in October 1944 when he was strongly tempted to pray for help.

> Naked and compressed among my naked companions with my index card in hand, I was waiting to file past the "commission" that would with one glance decide whether I should go immediately to the gas chamber or was instead strong enough to go on working. For one instant I felt the need to ask for help and asylum: then despite my anguish, equanimity prevailed: you do not change the rules of the game at the end of the match. . . . A prayer under these conditions would have been not only absurd . . . but blasphemous . . . . I rejected the temptation: I knew that if I were to survive, I would have to be ashamed of it (Wood, 96).

A human being facing the prospect of death or a future not worth living has few choices. The principal options are: 1) to appeal to God, history, or some other external source for hope and understanding; 2) to sink into despair; 3) to affirm life and self in the teeth of misfortune. If one is a non-believer and refuses the first option, then affirming life and self seems preferable to sinking into despair. Of course, a theist might see this as a missed opportunity to come to faith. The poet T. S. Eliot (1888-1965) scorned the third option as a desperate attempt to cheer oneself up. But atheists, like Camus and Levi, can reply that appealing to God when one has no compelling reason to believe in God is a far more desperate attempt to cheer oneself up.

For people who are not threatened with destruction, Camus' recipe may provide a lesson in making the most of life's passing moments. The fact that the ideal of "seizing the day" is still often called by its Latin name, "*carpe diem*," serves to remind us that writers and philosophers have been proposing this ideal since antiquity. Yet seizing the day is difficult to do. Even on good days, we are easily distracted from enjoying the present by regrets about the past, worries about the future, doubts about what others may think, and intrusive passions such as envy, jealousy, resentment, and obsessive desires. Pascal claimed that people focus on the present moment to avoid thinking about death and eternity, but, in fact, most people are not very good at focusing on the present moment. Camus' stirring words on living without appeal might help us to do this more successfully.

Ironically, this good advice also points to the weakest link in Camus' argument: his notion that we ought to disregard the future. "The absurd," he says, "enlightens me on this point: there is no future" (Camus, *Myth*, 1955, 43). "The ideal of the absurd man," he asserts, "is the present and the succession of presents" (Camus, *Myth*, 1955, 47). Yet this notion is misguided in two ways. First, there *is* a future, even if our individual futures are finite. Second, we can never completely disregard the future. As Heidegger and Sartre argued, human existence is inescapably temporal. For example, the simple act of signing one's name on a check involves a multiple-step projection into the future. I write each letter of my name in anticipation of the next letter in order to complete a signature which will authorize the cashing of this check to make a payment on my car so that I can get to work, etc., etc. Even a person as focused on the present as Meursault cannot escape this level of temporal projection, but for most people the future plays a larger and more elaborate role in giving meaning to the present.

It is telling that Camus picks Sisyphus in the underworld as the mythic embodiment of absurd heroism. Sisyphus in the underworld is a man who has lost his future. His existence *is* "the present and the endless succession of presents," but there is nothing ideal about it. Neither does his existence bear much resemblance to that of living human beings. Camus writes "that the workman of today works everyday in his life at the same tasks, and this fate is no less absurd" (Camus, *Myth*, 1955, 90). Yet this comparison is misleading. The life of a workman, like any other human life, gathers meaning from a multitude of little futures. However repetitive his labor, a workman usually looks forward to completing the task at hand: filling a pothole, for example, or loading a truck. He looks forward to collecting his paycheck, an evening meal, beer at the tavern, Sundays off. Perhaps, he dreams of buying his own house or sending his children to college. There may not be a grand theme or purpose to a workman's life, but that life is enriched by change, variety, and fellowship with others. If illness or misfortune makes *his* life (not life itself) unbearable, he, unlike Sisyphus, has the option of suicide. However brief and poor his life may be, it is still richer than the fate of Sisyphus.

5
Camus the Moralist

A. Deficiencies of an Absurdist Morality

Readers of Camus who equate his views on morality with what he wrote before 1943 are likely to have a distorted picture of what he came to believe about right and wrong during the last sixteen years of his life. As I noted in previous chapters, both *The Stranger* and *Caligula* leave moral questions hanging. Meursault is condemned to death on the absurd pretext that he is a "monster" who is "morally guilty of killing his mother," and yet he has taken another man's life without any intelligible reason for doing so and feels no remorse. What are we to think of Meursault in moral terms? Caligula murders and torments his subjects in his quest for the "impossible." Although he finally admits that he has taken the wrong path, it is not clear whether this is an admission of moral failure or metaphysical miscalculation.

Since *The Stranger* and *Caligula* are fictional works in which character and story line are more important than arguments, this ambiguity does not disrupt their integrity and may, in fact, add to their fascination. The same cannot be said for *The Myth of Sisyphus*. Although literary essays are not as tightly bound to rational arguments as philosophical essays, they do depend on arguments for clarity and coherence, and Camus' arguments about morality (or ethics) in *The Myth of Sisyphus* are logically muddled.

For example, in *The Myth of Sisyphus*, Camus cites a famous passage from Fyodor Dostoyevsky's great novel *The Brothers Karamazov* in which one of the brothers, Ivan, claims that if there is no God or immortality, then everything is permitted. Ivan's ideas about God and morality are closely tied to issues of immortality, but Camus, like Sartre, prefers to drop the reference to immortality and use the proposition "If there is no God, then everything is permitted" as a point of departure for talking about the moral consequences of a universe without divine or transcendent values.

What exactly does it mean to say: "If God does not exist, then everything would be *permitted*"? It cannot mean that God permits every action, since the if-clause (antecedent) of this if-then (conditional) proposition assumes that God does not exist. Neither is there anything in this simple proposition to suggest that the "permitting" is done by some other agency—government, or society, for example. The term "permitted" in this proposition has a meaning that is common in philosophical ethics although less common in everyday discussion. It means "not wrong" or "not forbidden." A basic distinction in ethics is between wrong acts and acts that are *either* obligatory (acts one ought to do) or optional (acts one may do). What makes wrong acts different from obligatory and optional acts is that they are acts that one ought *not* to do: they are morally forbidden acts. Now, if one believes that moral rightness (what one ought to do) and moral wrongness (what one ought not to do) depend entirely on God, then the non-existence of God would imply that nothing is morally forbidden.

Surprisingly, Camus gets confused on this point. He writes in *The Myth of Sisyphus*:

> The absurd does not liberate, it binds. It does not authorize all actions. "Everything is permitted" does not mean that nothing is forbidden. [*Tous sont permis ne signifie pas que rien n'est défendu.*] (Camus, *Myth*, 1955, 50, *Essais*, 1965, 149).

What Camus confuses is the meaning of the clause "everything is permitted" with his belief that despite the absence of God or any other external moral order in the world, there are some actions that one ought not to do—in other words, actions that are wrong or forbidden. What Camus should have said is that the entire conditional proposition "If God does not exist, then everything is forbidden" is false.

Perhaps, Camus slips on this logical point because he stakes out his own position on philosophically shaky ground. Although Camus advocates atheism, he embraces a narrowly theistic view on formal ethics: "There is but one moral code (*une morale*) that the absurd man can accept, the one that is not separated from God: the one that is dictated. But it so happens, that he lives outside that God" (Camus, *Myth*, 1955, 49). As a consequence, he forces himself into the position of having to make an informal and subjective case against actions and attitudes he considers to be wrong.

For example, he argues: "The absurd confers an equivalence on the consequences of . . . actions. It does not recommend crime, for this would be childish, but it restores to remorse its futility" (Camus, *Myth*, 1955, 50). Yet this is not convincing. While it may be true that in the long run we will all be dead with no eternal God to pass judgments on our actions, in the short run the consequences of our actions are far from equivalent. An armed robber who shoots a teenager and causes her to be paralyzed for life produces morally different consequences from someone who does her no harm. Remorse may be futile in the sense that it doesn't help victims or possess intrinsic moral worth, but genuine remorse is a sign and source of reform. Other things being equal, people who feel remorseful about what they have done are less likely to do it again than people who lack remorse.

As for not recommending crime because it is "childish," this is probably a reference to surrealists like André Bréton. Bréton once gave as an example of a surrealist act walking down the street with a pistol and shooting people at random in a crowd. But unless ethical grounds can be offered for choosing one course of action over another, a surrealist could reasonably insist that acting childishly is no worse than acting maturely and killing people is no worse than helping them.

Camus also argues that in the absence of an external moral order "the absurd mind cannot so much expect ethical rules at the end of its reasoning as, rather, illustrations and the breath of human lives" (Camus, *Myth*, 1955, 50). The point here seems to be that ethics in the face of absurdity must take the form of "situation ethics" in which illustrations and loosely formulated ideals (e.g. lucidity, revolt, freedom, and passion) take the place of ethical rules and systems. This point is consistent with the outlook adopted a little later by Jean-Paul Sartre in his famous lecture in 1945 "Existentialism is a Humanism" and by Simone de Beauvoir in her book *The Ethics of Ambiguity* (1946), but this point does not absolve Camus, Sartre, Beauvoir, or any other situation ethicist of the need to defend the ideals they put forward and show how they could be used as practical guides to action.

In *The Myth of Sisyphus*, Camus attempts to illustrate how people in different walks of life can face the absurd without hope or illusion by presenting sketches of the seducer, the actor, and the conqueror. Unfortunately, these sketches offer no practical guidance. Their virtues are the ones that Camus has already celebrated: lucidity, passion, revolt, etc. Rather than providing criteria and arguments for distinguishing what is more or less admirable in their conduct and condemning their vices, Camus asserts: "Neither I nor anybody else can judge them here" (Camus, *Myth* 1955, 67).

One reason for Camus' reluctance to "judge" may be his recognition that ethical rules (or principles) conflict in some cases with other ethical rules or with people's feelings about what is right and wrong. Ethical rules such as "don't kill," "don't steal," and "don't lie," are taught in one form or another by virtually every society, and yet it is easy to think of situations where violating these rules would seem to make more sense than obeying it. If the only way I can save an innocent life is by lying to a murderer, then I probably ought to lie.

Of course, not all ethical rules are as vulnerable to exceptions as this one. The Golden Rule and similar principles of universalizability (i.e. treating people in morally comparable the same way) hold up rather well. Moreover, we can improve universalizability by allowing for morally relevant differences, such as whether a person is an adult or a child. Yet even if every ethical rule fails sometimes, it does not follow that we can get along without them. Camus is mistaken when he says, "I note everyday that integrity has no need of rules" (Camus *Myth*, 1955, 49). There are instances where one's sense of integrity or feelings about right or wrong may not be strong or clear enough to afford adequate guidance. This is often the case when has to choose the lesser of two evils. W. D. Ross, a twentieth century British philosopher, promoted the idea of "prima facie" duties. A prima facie duty is something one ought to do, unless there are compelling reasons for not doing it. An ethical rule that succeeded in identifying a true prima facie duty would provide a great deal of guidance, even though it did not provide invariable guidance. Hence, there is an attractive middle ground between invariable rules and loosely ethical formulated ideals on the other hand. Camus failed to see this middle ground, and, therefore, missed a chance to give his ethical views a better formulation.

B. Resistance: *Letters to a German Friend*

Significantly, neither Camus, nor Sartre, nor Beauvoir remained satisfied for long with their efforts to construct and defend a strictly situational approach to ethics. Sartre and Beauvoir drifted towards Marxism. Camus rejected Marxism and drifted toward an impassioned but philosophically vague affirmation of justice and happiness. The turning point in Camus' thinking about morality coincided with his active involvement in the French Resistance. Although he had always despised Fascism and Nazism, he did not translate that aversion into ethical terms until he was personally confronted with the brutality of Nazism and the opportunity to do something about it. In 1943, Camus agreed to serve as editor-in-chief of a Resistance newspaper at first called *La Revue Noire*, but soon renamed *Combat*. *Combat* proclaimed that it had one leader, Charles de Gaulle, and one goal: to "fight for our freedoms." By late 1943, 250,000 copies were printed of each issue. Working for *Combat* was a dangerous business in Nazi-occupied France. The printer who produced *Combat*, André Bollier, committed suicide just as he was about to be arrested by the Germans. He knew that he would be tortured to reveal the names of other Resistants. Although Camus was never involved in military operations for the Resistance, he, too, ran the risk of torture, execution, or imprisonment in a concentration camp.

In the summer of 1943, Camus began writing a series of four anonymous letters to an imaginary German friend for publication in other Resistance journals. Two were published clandestinely before the liberation of Paris; all four appeared after the war as a little book entitled *Letters to a German Friend*. What is most notable about these letters is their *lack* of moral ambiguity. In the opening paragraph of the first letter, Camus "replies" to his friend's declaration that anything is good that contributes to his country's greatness, with a firm response:

> I cannot believe that everything must be subordinated to a single end. There are means that cannot be excused. And I should like to be able to love my country and still love justice. I don't want any greatness for it, particularly a greatness born of blood and falsehood (Camus, *RRD*, 1960, 5).

Camus goes on to contrast a Germany that had prepared itself for conquest by making violence more natural than thinking with a France that had been ill-prepared to thwart the German onslaught because it had to overcome its loathing for war, its idea of a higher civilization, its concern for justice. "It took us all that time to find out if we had the right to kill men, if we were allowed to add to the frightful misery of the world" (Camus, *RRD*, 1960, 8). While this line of argument is too simplistic and idealistic to serve as a historical explanation for France's humiliating defeat by Germany in 1940, it works quite well as a moral comparison between a totalitarian society in which everything is subordinated to national destiny and a pluralistic society in which humane values and independent thinking are respected. Between these alternatives Camus does not hesitate. There is no hint here that he cannot judge who is right and who is wrong.

Another striking difference between *Letters to a German Friend* and Camus' previous work is the emphasis he gives in these letters to solidarity. In his previous work, he had focused on the plight of the individual confronted by a world without God, hope, or meaning. Like Pascal, he tended to treat "the society of others" as a diversion from the fundamental challenge of existence. Again like Pascal, he used the loneliness of the condemned prisoner as a paradigm for the human condition. But in *Letters to a German Friend* he treats voluntary commitment to a common cause as a source of meaning and value. Here he writes of "a Frenchman workman walking toward the guillotine at dawn . . . and exhorting his comrades from cell to cell to show their courage" (Camus, *RRD*, 1960, 8).

In a particularly revealing passage, Camus tells his German friend that before the war he, too, was inclined to "deduce" from the meaninglessness of the world: "the idea that everything was equivalent and that good and evil could be defined according to one's wishes" (Camus, *RRD*, 1960, 27). The difference, he explains, was:

> Simply that you saw the injustice of our condition to the point of being willing to add to it, whereas it seemed to me that man must exalt justice in order to fight against injustice, create happiness in order to protest against a universe of unhappiness . . . I merely wanted men to rediscover their solidarity in order to wage war against their revolting fate (Camus, *RRD*, 1960, 27-28).

Camus goes on to say that while the world itself has no ultimate meaning, "man has meaning, because he is the only creature to insist on having one. This world has at least the truth of man . . . ." (Camus, *RRD*, 1960, 28). Translated into the language of ethical theory, Camus seems to be endorsing a "naturalistic" position along the following lines: "Since it is natural for human being to desire justice and happiness despite the world's indifference to these desires, human beings ought to band together to fight injustice and create happiness."

A few days after the liberation of Paris in August 1944, Camus wrote an editorial on the new role he expected *Combat* to play: "We have decided to suppress politics and replace it with morality" (Todd, 195). By "morality" he seems to have meant what ethical theorists call "a moral point of view." But even if one takes a moral point of view, it can still be difficult to decide specific moral issues. One of the first moral issues to confront French intellectuals after the war was the sentencing of writers and journalists who had collaborated with the Nazis. Sartre and Beauvoir, like many intellectuals on the political left, favored the death penalty for writers who had abetted or endorsed the murders of the Nazi regime. François Mauriac, a Catholic novelist who had been active in the Resistance, called for charity and reconciliation. Camus attempted to steer a middle course, demanding justice for collaborators who had abetted or endorsed murder while agonizing over the use of the death penalty to punish them. In some cases, Camus saw justice in execution; in other cases, he petitioned for clemency. By 1948, however, he admitted publicly that Mauriac had been right.

C. Fighting Evil: *The Plague*

In the aftermath of World War II, Camus became convinced that it is easier to discover how to fight evil than it is to discover how to transform society to make it more successful at producing good. He came to believe that our hearts and minds (if they have not been warped) inform us that death, suffering, injustice, and slavery are evil and that life, happiness, justice, and freedom are good. Thus, to the extent that we can prevent or diminish death, suffering, injustice, and oppression, we can make this indifferent world a better place. But when we try to reason beyond the confines of our own history and experience to create a new and better social order, we run the risk, not only of being mistaken, but of causing death, suffering, injustice and oppression in the course of our efforts to promote the good. Therefore, Camus concluded, we ought to act in solidarity to fight these evils, but proceed with caution in attempting to promote good by transforming society so that we become neither victims nor executioners.

This line of thinking is remarkable both for its confident attitude toward morality and for its cautious attitude toward radical political change. It is reminiscent of the "conservative" views of Edmund Burke, an Irish/British philosopher of the late 1700's who defended the Irish independence movement and the rebellion of American colonies, but opposed the French revolution. Interestingly, Burke's views stemmed in part from his religious convictions that evil is unavoidable and humanity cannot be "perfected" by reason. Camus' views on fighting evil are exemplified with power and style in *The Plague*. His views on revolt and revolution are presented less successfully in the meandering arguments of *The Rebel*.

The Plague is an allegorical novel. Read as straightforward narrative, it tells a fictional story about an outbreak of bubonic plague in the Algerian port city of Oran from April 16, 194_ until the next February. Read on a metaphorical plane, it presents a matrix of moral options (fighting, running, altruism, selfishness, etc.) that human beings can exercise when confronted with pervasive but unpredictable evil and traces some of the probable consequences of exercising those options. The specific evil in the fictional story is the bubonic plagues, but one can easily imagine other evils that would work as well on the metaphorical plane, evils such the Nazi occupation of Europe or the oppression of people by their "own" totalitarian dictatorships.

The main character of *The Plague* is Dr. Bernard Rieux, a physician from a working-class family who lives and practices medicine in Oran. At the end of the novel, Rieux reveals that he is also the story's third person narrator and claims that he has concealed his authorship until the end in order to maintain the role of a witness giving testimony. This explanation is consistent with the even tone of the novel and its journalistic perspectives on events, but the late revelation of Rieux's authorship may also serve to delay and blunt readers' suspicions about his objectivity in describing himself. Rieux presents himself as a man who has resolved "to have no truck with injustice and compromises with truth" (Camus, *Plague* 1948, 12) and nothing that happens in the novel contradicts this claim.

In point of honesty, Rieux resembles Meursault, but unlike the self-absorbed Meursault he cares about the welfare of others and is committed to the humane objectives of his profession. There is nothing starry-eyed or sanctimonious about Rieux; he is well aware of the moral frailties of his patients and limitations of his craft. His mission as a doctor is to fight against suffering and death—though he knows that death will always prevail. In this respect, he resembles Sisyphus, and that resemblance is thrown into high relief by the rising death tolls of the bubonic plague. Talking to his friend Jean Tarrou, Rieux asks:

> "[M]ightn't it be better for God if we refuse to believe in him and struggle with all our might against death, without raising our eyes toward the heaven where He sits in silence." . . . "Yes, I know that. But it's no reason for giving up the struggle." "No reason, I agree. Only, I now can picture what this plague must mean for you." "Yes, a never ending defeat" (Camus, *Plague*, 1948, 117-118).

However, Rieux is doing more than Sisyphus. In addition to scorning the gods and affirming himself, in addition to giving meaning to the successive moments of his own existence, he is also doing his best to secure slightly longer and better futures for other people.

Rieux's explanation for his moral outlook stresses the centrality of moral knowledge and ignorance. He says:

> On the whole, men are more good than bad; that, however, isn't the real point. But they are more or less ignorant; and it is this that we call vice and virtue; the most incorrigible vice being that of an ignorance that fancies it knows everything and therefore claims for itself the right to kill (Camus, *Plague*, 1948, 120-121).

This comes close to Socrates' twofold view: 1) people always do what they believe to be good; 2) those who know the good will do the good. Indeed, Rieux goes on to compare the commitment of the sanitary squads to that of a school teacher who teaches that two plus two equals four. He explains their resolve to fight the plague and save as many people as possible, whatever the risk to their own safety, as a matter of necessity. "This truth was not admirable, it was only consistent" (Camus, *TRN* 1962, 1325). What Rieux does not explain is *how* they knew this was "the good."

Rieux's determination to fight suffering and death is shared from the outset by three other characters: the mysterious Jean Tarrou, who creates the sanitary squads, Joseph Grand, a frail clerk and would-be writer who works each night to keep their records, and Dr. Castel, an elderly physician who labors to produce an effective serum against the plague. Although each, in his own way, is something of a hero, Tarrou is the only one for whom heroism (or sainthood as he prefers to call it) is a self-conscious objective.

In some ways, Tarrou is like the itinerant hero of an American Western who rides into town at a moment of crisis to help the townspeople defend themselves against a dangerous foe. He arrives in Oran just a few weeks before the plague appears, takes a room in a big hotel and quickly establishes a wide circle of acquaintances. Although a relatively young man, he has no visible means of support. No one knows where he has come from or what brought him to Oran. When the plague breaks out, it is Tarrou who draws up a plan for voluntary groups of helpers to do the dirty work necessary to help contain the plague. Rieux tells him his chance of surviving will be one in three, but Tarrou shrugs that off with a story about a city in Persia where the only survivor of a plague was the man who washed the corpses. As director of the sanitary squads, Tarrou does as much—perhaps more— than the medical professionals to fight the plague. His zeal never flags, until he himself is stricken with the plague and dies.

Two months or so before his death, Tarrou tells Rieux about his past. He says that he came from a prosperous family and that his father was a prosecuting attorney. As a teenager, he had all of the gifts and advantages for which one might wish. His parents were kind. He was smart, successful with young women, and not too scrupulous about his moral lapses. One day his father brought him to court, and he watched his father, dressed in a red robe, use his eloquence to demand the death penalty for a criminal. Although the defendant more or less admitted his guilt, young Tarrou was horrified by the spectacle of the State condemning a pathetic and frightened man to death. About a year later, he left home. He became a political agitator and a member of an international group, whose name he does not specify (probably a Communist organization). For years, he participated in political struggles throughout Europe—trying all the while not to dwell on the "justified" killings *his* side was committing. One day in Hungary he witnessed a man being executed by firing squad. His sense of horror returned and he vowed to avoid "anything which, directly or indirectly, for good reasons or for bad, brings death to anyone or justifies others putting him to death" (Camus, *Plague*, 1948, 228-229).

Tarrou also explains his moral outlook in conceptual terms. Since he believes that our troubles spring from failure to use plain, clean-cut, language, he is always very careful to speak and act with clarity. He tells Rieux that the world is divided into scourges (*les fléaux*), victims, and true healers (*les vrais médecins*). Because the last are very rare, he concentrates on taking the victim's side and never becoming a willful murderer. But Tarrou also has less modest goals: he hopes to attain peace by following "the path of sympathy," and he aspires "to be a saint without God" (Camus, *Plague*, 1948, 230). Although these goals are not analyzed in *The Plague*, it is reasonable to suppose that they involve a commitment to the welfare of others that goes beyond the call of duty. In practical terms, this aspiration to be a secular saint may be reflected in Tarrou's willingness to roam the world in search of victims to help, while Rieux remains at home trying to balance his private life with a steady commitment to fight death and suffering.

Although *The Plague* has no villains and practically no politics, it has several characters who serve as ethical foils to the atheistic humanism of Rieux and Tarrou and the solidarity of the plague fighters whom they lead. Among these foils, the most notable are Raymond Rambert and Father Paneloux.

Rambert is a journalist who has come from France to write an exposé on the bad living conditions in the Arab quarter of Oran. When the plague breaks out, a strict quarantine is imposed on the city and he is not permitted to leave. In addition to the danger and unpleasantness of living in a plague-ridden city, Rambert suffers intensely from being separated from the woman he loves in Paris. (Camus, who lived in Paris during the occupation, was cut off from his new wife, Francine, after the allied invasion of North Africa.) As a stranger to Oran, with no aspirations to be a saint, he conspires to end his exile by being smuggled out of the city. Rambert is no coward: he fought as a volunteer in the Spanish civil war. But now he wants to put love before duty or sympathy.

In a poignant exchange with Rieux and Tarrou, Rambert declares: "I don't believe in heroism. I know it's easy and I've learned it can be murderous. What interests me is living and dying for what one loves" (Camus, *Plague*, 1948, 149). Rieux protests that it is not heroism but common decency that motivates him, but he adds "you are *not* wrong to put love first" (Camus, *Plague*, 1948, 150). What Rieux (and Camus)

75

seem to believe is that acting out of love for an individual is as valid an ethical priority as acting out of sympathy for human suffering. But Rambert misunderstands Rieux's point and quips: "I suppose you have nothing to lose" (Camus, *Plague*, 1948, 150). After Rieux is gone, Tarrou tells Rambert that Rieux's sick wife is in a sanatorium hundreds of miles away. Early the next morning Rambert volunteers to work with Rieux. Although his chance to escape eventually arrives, he does not leave Oran until the quarantine is lifted. At the end of the novel, he is reunited with his lover. Rieux, whose wife has died, wonders whether she might have lived if he had been able to care for her.

Father Paneloux represents a very different moral outlook. Like Saint Augustine, he believes that all of the evils in this world are the result of sin and just punishment for sin and that God unfailingly transforms evil into good. He sees in this plague the flail (*le fléau*) of God scourging the citizens of Oran for their lack of devotion while, at the same time, pointing the way to eternal salvation. In his first sermon on the plague, Paneloux draws an implicit line between himself and his audience. He repeatedly uses the word 'you' (*vous*) to identify those who have provoked God into allowing (though not willing) this plague to happen. "Calamity has come on you, my brethren, and my brethren you deserved it" (Camus, *Plague*, 1948, 86-87). Instead of expressing sympathy for the suffering of his neighbors, he blasts them with righteous indignation and tells them the plague is a blessing in disguise. He exhorts his audience to "rejoice" and describes a long-ago outbreak plague in Abyssinia where Christians who were *not* infected wrapped themselves in the sheets of plague victims in order to ensure their own death. "No doubt," he adds, "this frenzy is not to be commended . . . But, nonetheless, this example teaches its lesson" (Camus, *TRN*, 1962, 1297). Concluding in the same vein, he asserts that "Never more than today, had Father Paneloux felt the divine help and Christian hope that was being offered to everyone" (Camus, *TRN*, 1962, 1297-1298.)

Some weeks later, Tarrou asks Paneloux to join the sanitary squads, and he agrees. He devotes himself to working with plague victims in the hospitals, where the risk of infection is particularly high. In the most vivid scene in the novel, Paneloux and Rieux come together to watch an attempt to save the life of a boy stricken with the plague by using Dr. Castel's new serum. The serum has little or no effect, and the boy dies slowly in horrible agony. Paneloux seeks to find some common ground with Rieux in dealing with this tragedy, but Rieux declares that he cannot accept a scheme of things in which children are put to torture.

It is against this background that Paneloux gives his second sermon. In a gentler voice and less confident manner, he addresses his audience, using the word 'we' (*nous*) instead of 'you' (*vous*). He tells them he still believes what he said in his previous sermon, but that his words and thoughts had lacked charity. He goes on to say that good and evil are usually easy to distinguish and understand. We can understand, for example, why a seducer, like Don Juan, was cast into hell. But other events, like the death of a child, surpass human understanding. Up to this point Paneloux's words are conventional, but he suddenly turns in a direction that echoes the debates of the Karamazov brothers. He knows it would be comforting to believe that the death of a child is compensated by eternal happiness in heaven, but he cannot be sure that heavenly happiness can make up for human suffering. Rather than look for such explanations, he chooses to keep faith with the tortured body of Christ and to insist that in times such as these one must accept all or nothing. In other words, one must have faith that everything is an expression of God's love or give up trying to be a Christian.

After the sermon, an old priest remarks to a young deacon who is leaving the church with him that Paneloux displayed "more uneasiness than real power" (Camus, *Plague*, 1948, 206). The deacon confides that Paneloux is working on an even bolder essay that questions whether it is logical for a priest to consult a doctor. When Paneloux becomes ill a few days later, he waits as long as possible before calling a doctor, finally he calls Rieux to comply with the regulations. He is taken to the hospital, where he dies holding his crucifix. Earlier Rieux had told Tarrou that no one in the world, not even Paneloux, believed in an all-powerful God and "this was proved by the fact that no one ever threw himself on Providence completely" (Camus, *Plague*, 1948, 116). Paneloux proves him wrong.

What are the principal lessons of this allegorical novel? The first is the recurrence of plagues and wars. The first time the word 'plague' is uttered in this novel, Rieux remarks: "There have been as many plagues as wars in history; yet always plagues and wars take people by surprise" (Camus, *Plague* 1948, 34). This is true. Most people think of plagues and wars, if they remember them at all, as artifacts of the past. Few people today know that the influenza epidemic of 1918-1919 caused over 20 million deaths worldwide, and fewer still could have guessed that a worldwide epidemic in their own time (AIDS) would kill

77

an even larger number of people. (According to UNAIDS, 18.8 million had died of AIDS by June 1999 and 34.8 million were infected with HIV/AIDS.) A second lesson is that in time of plague (occupation, or similar calamities), most people will concentrate on protecting themselves and their families, trying to maintain "normal" lives, and dreaming about a plague-free future. *The Plague* does not imply that this self-centeredness is contemptible. A few people, however, will put personal advantage aside and join together to fight a common evil— whether or not they share a common ideology. The third lesson is that those who choose to fight may never know whether their efforts and sacrifices made a real difference. Plagues usually end as mysteriously as they begin. All one can know for sure is that victory over plague and other forms of terror is never final.

D. Rebellion and Revolution: *The Rebel*

The Rebel (*L'Homme révolté*) was published in 1951, four years after *The Plague*. Not since *Christian Metaphysics and Neo-Platonism*, had Camus attempted to write a philosophical study grounded in historical scholarship. The writing of this book was prompted in part by changes in global politics. The end-of-the-war alliance of Britain, France, and the United States with the Soviet Union quickly dissolved into the Cold War between the Soviet Bloc and a broader Western alliance. The euphoria of victory over Germany and Japan was soon replaced by fears of a Third World War with atomic weapons and a Soviet invasion of Western Europe. In 1948, the Soviet Union blockaded the roads to West Berlin and instigated a communist coup in Czechoslovakia. The U.S. overcame the blockade with a massive airlift. It also provided help for the rebuilding of Western Europe through the Marshall Plan. In 1949, the Soviets tested their first atomic bomb and celebrated the victory of Communist over the Nationalist forces in China. The U.S. sponsored the creation of NATO (The North Atlantic Treaty Organization) and undertook new rearmament programs. In 1950, the Cold War became a hot war, when (Communist) North Korea invaded South Korea. After gaining a quick endorsement from the United Nations' Security Council (the Soviets were absent), U.S. and allied troops pushed the North Koreans out of South Korea and marched as far as the Chinese border, provoking the

Chinese to enter the war. In America, the start of the Cold War led to anti-Communist crusades and made it difficult to defend any political program that was left of center. In France, the start of the Cold War led to bitter divisions across a much broader spectrum of political ideologies. The elections of 1951 left the French Assembly with most of its seats split fairly evenly among six political parties.

Sartre, Beauvoir, and most of their friends sided with the communists against capitalism and the Western bloc. Although not blind to the purges, political executions, and labor camps in the Soviet bloc, they underestimated the extent and severity of these "excesses" and believed that international communism was the only movement capable of defending the interests of workers and peasants around the world. Camus disagreed. He found the murderous brutality of the communist regimes unacceptable and believed that the Western bloc was the lesser of two evils. As the son of a working class family and former member of the Communist Party, he remained committed to ideals of social justice, but he believed that a society ought to promote personal and political liberties as well as social justice. He was offended by the spectacle of middle-class (bourgeois) intellectuals, like Sartre and his friends, urging workers to subordinate their freedom to the discipline of the Communist Party. He doubted whether intellectuals from comfortable and well-educated families untouched by poverty or illiteracy were in any position to speak on behalf of workers and peasants. For economic inspiration Camus looked to revolutionary trade-unionism. For political inspiration, Camus looked north and south rather than east and west. He was impressed by the framework of political liberalism and economic socialism that was being forged in the nations of Scandinavia. He reflected with pride on the moderation, earthiness, and lack of regimentation that he believed to be the spirit of the Mediterranean basin.

The Rebel is over three hundred pages and much of it is devoted to the discussion of selected cases of intellectual and/or political rebellion and revolution in Western history. I shall not try to cover all of these cases. Various critical works, including David Sprintzen's *Camus: A Critical Examination* (1988), contain handy summaries of these cases, but the cases themselves are clear, interesting, and quite easy to read. Here, as elsewhere, Camus was more comfortable with concrete examples than abstract reasoning.

In the "Introduction" to *The Rebel* Camus takes a hard look at his attempt to formulate an ethics of the absurd and pronounces it a failure.

He cites two reasons for this failure. First, it led to a contradiction concerning murder. Second, it was based on a "perception" (of the absurd) and "emotions" (of despair) that were particular to the period between the two World Wars rather than universal to humanity.

Although Camus does not succeed in demonstrating a logical contradiction concerning murder, he does point out an internal inconsistency between the absurd man's affirmation of his own life and what he owes to others. This inconsistency has the following form. On the one hand, a morality of the absurd makes "murder seem a matter of indifference. . . . if nothing has any meaning . . . then everything is possible and nothing has any importance . . . the murderer is neither right nor wrong" (Camus, *Rebel*, 1956, 5). On the other hand:

> The final conclusion of absurdist reasoning is in fact the repudiation of suicide and the acceptance of the desperate encounter between human inquiry and the silence of the universe. . . . But it is obvious that absurdism hereby admits that human life is the only necessary good since it is precisely life that makes this encounter possible . . . (Camus, *Rebel*, 1956, 6).

Camus' second reason for rejecting an ethics of the absurd is external criticism. He charges that the perception of the absurd and the emotions of despair this perception aroused were too selective to provide an adequate basis for rules of action. They were, he suggests, the intellectual obsession of a particular period in European history. "The error of a whole period of history has been to enunciate . . . general rules of action founded on emotions of despair . . ." (Camus, *Rebel*, 1956, 9). World War I led to an "age of negation" that focused attention on suicide. World War II, has led to an "age of ideologies" that raised the question of murder. "We shall know nothing until we know whether we have the right to kill our fellow men, or the right to let them be killed" (Camus, *Rebel*, 1956, 4).

It is ironic that having shaken off the overly selective viewpoint of the absurd, Camus should now encumber himself with the category of rebellion (*la révolte*). (Note that the French '*la révolte*' can be translated as 'revolt' or 'rebellion.'). Although 'rebellion,' unlike 'the absurd' is a descriptive category of human action with no particular philosophical significance, it is at once too broad and too narrow to serve as an appropriate point of departure for ethical inquiry. It is too broad because there is no persuasive basis for claiming that rebellion itself is right or wrong. What makes a rebellion right or wrong are its goals, motives, tactics, or consequences, not the fact that it is a rebellion. This category is too narrow because ideological terror and murder can arise from established power as well as from revolutionary fervor. It is also too narrow to contain with much grace the array of literary and philosophical figures that Camus discusses in *The Rebel*.

Why did Camus choose the category of rebellion? Probably, for three reasons. First, he wanted to salvage something positive from his earlier attempt to devise a morality of the absurd. Although absurdist reasoning failed to answer the question of murder, it offered the revolt of the absurd hero as a positive point of departure. Second, Camus had discovered his own dissatisfaction with ethical nihilism (the belief that there are no objective ethical values) and the importance of solidarity through his participation in the French Resistance. He knew from experience what it was like to rebel against oppression. Third, he preferred to anchor his ethical vision in dramatic imagery. He had learned this lesson from his teacher Jean Grenier, and it was to Grenier that he dedicated *The Rebel*.

What is a rebel? In Part One of *The Rebel*, Camus explains rebellion (or revolt) as a refusal of authority, which at the same time affirms new values. "A slave who has taken orders all his life suddenly decides that he cannot obey some new command" (Camus, *Rebel*, 1956, 13). It is not merely that he wants to avoid obeying this command; he might do that by lying or trickery. The slave *refuses* to obey, and in refusing sets a limit beyond which he or she will not go. Setting this limit implicitly invokes a moral value, principle, or right. The slave may be implying that there are some things even a slave should not be ordered to do, or, more radically, that slavery itself is wrong and she will no longer obey. This moral value, principle, or right is also a foundation for solidarity with others. For a slave to affirm that "no slave should be ordered to give up her children" or "no human being should be a slave" [my examples] is to make common cause with others who share her condition, and, by extension, with humanity. In this sense, rebellion implies solidarity with other human beings. René Descartes declared "I think, therefore I am"; Camus declares "I rebel—therefore, we exist." (Camus, *Rebel* 1956, 22).

But rebellion is a risky business. In most cases, oppressors do not give up without a fight. Thus, a rebel is likely to be faced with a choice to kill or be killed. To kill is to deny one's common humanity. "If a

81

single master should, in fact, be killed the rebel . . . is no longer justified in using the term *community of men* from which he derived his justification" (Camus, *Rebel*, 1956, 281). To be killed is to yield to one's oppressor. For Camus, this is the fundamental dilemma of rebellion. "If [rebels] retreat they must accept death, if they advance they must accept murder" (Camus, *Rebel* 1956, 281). In either case rebellion is betrayed. One piece of Camus' proposed solution to this dilemma is the curious thesis that rebels who kill should be prepared to die in atonement for their violation of human solidarity. In his 1949 play *The Just Assassins* (*Les Justes*), Camus used Ivan Kaliayev, the poet-revolutionary, to embody this conviction.

In Part Two, "Metaphysical Rebellion," Camus returns to the religious roots of his philosophical thought. He characterizes metaphysical rebellion as "the movement by which man protests against his condition and against the whole of creation" (Camus, *Rebel*, 1956, 26). Although he insists that metaphysical rebellion does not appear in coherent form until the end of the eighteenth century, he sees anticipations as far back as the myth of Prometheus. According to Greek legend, the titan Prometheus stole fire from the Olympian gods to give humans warmth and light. As punishment for his rebellion, and his refusal to seek forgiveness, Zeus had him chained at the end of the earth, where each day an eagle (or vulture) came to tear out his liver. Camus' switch from Sisyphus to Prometheus is telling: Sisyphus defied the gods in service to himself, Prometheus in service to humankind.

Camus also finds anticipations of metaphysical rebellion in Christ, the Christian Gnostics, and Saint Augustine. Yet as long as Christianity dominated Western thought, it offered an alternative to rebellion: redemption through the voluntary suffering of an innocent God. It was only when Christ's divinity was called into question in the eighteenth century that metaphysical rebellion came into to its own. Among the figures that make up Camus' parade of metaphysical rebels are the Marquis de Sade, the characters of Satan in Milton's *Paradise Lost* and Ivan in Dostoyevsky's *The Brothers Karamazvov*, the French poets Baudelaire, Lautréament, Rimbaud, Breton, and, two German philosophers Max Stirner (1806-1856) and Nietzsche. Camus finds at the core of metaphysical rebellion protest against unjustified evil and suffering and a demand for unity. If God cannot or will not abolish unjustified evil and suffering, then it is up to humans to do so. Thus, according to Camus, metaphysical rebellion leads to revolution.

In Part Three, "Historical Rebellion," Camus explores the

relationship between rebellion and revolution ('*la révolte*' and '*la révolution*'). He argues that revolution is "the injection of ideas into historical experience, while rebellion is only the movement that leads from individual experience into the realm of ideas" (Camus, *Rebel*, 1956, 26). Rebellion awakens values, solidarity, and a demand for unity, while revolution seeks to remake the world in their image. Rebellion demands unity; revolution demands totality.

Although Part Three occupies nearly half of *The Rebel*, the number of revolutions Camus examines is surprisingly small. He examines the French Revolution (1789-1799), revolutionary activity in Czarist Russia (1820-1916), the Bolshevik (Russian) Revolution (1917-1920), and the Fascist quasi-revolutions in Italy and German (1921-1945). He also discusses the ideas of Hegel, Nietzsche, and especially Marx. To justify this selectivity, Camus insists that the true "spirit of rebellion" requires two conditions that occur only in modern (post-1750) Western society. One condition is theoretical equality among people. The other is a rejection of the sacred. On this basis he sets aside rebellions of slaves, serfs, peasants, nationalists, religious reformers, and non-Western revolutions such as Gandhi's remarkable non-violent revolution in India after World War II. He also leaves himself unable to deal with the American Civil War. He bypasses the American Revolution with the facile assertion: "1789 completes the conquests of the English and American revolutions" (Camus, *Rebel*, 1956, 281).

Why did Camus do this? I suspect the main reasons were his habit of seeing the world through the lens of his "Christian preoccupations" and his lack of familiarity with the history of nations outside of continental Europe. Perhaps, he was also to trying to take a Hegelian approach to history by teasing out those strands that best fit his ideological preconceptions. G. W. Hegel (1770-1831) was an ingeniously original philosopher who developed a dialectical logic (a logic of thesis, antithesis, and synthesis) to trace the essential ideas that define reality. Hegel also bent reality to fit his ideas. For example, he omitted Islam from his history of religion because it came after Christianity and, hence, failed to fit his dialectical account of how the spirit of reason progressed through cultural history. It was Hegel who inspired Karl Marx (1818-1883) to see history as a dialectical progression. Although Camus is very critical of Hegel in *The Rebel* for pretending to capture the totality of history, Camus may have failed to see that the devil of Hegelian arrogance is also in the details.

Camus' principal targets in *The Rebel* are Marxism and Soviet communism. He finds in the former a profound example of how reason in search of totality can betray itself. He finds in the latter a horrifying example of how the generous spirit of rebellion can be twisted into a totalitarian nightmare. Camus is unsparing. He faults each step in the evolution of Soviet communism.

Camus' criticizes Karl Marx for treating history as a closed system. Marx explained history as an inevitable progression from the primitive communism of tribal societies to the development of economic classes and class warfare to a final victory of the working class (which Marx called "the proletariat") and the emergence of a global and technology advanced classless society. Camus mocks this explanation as an attempt to rewrite a Christian view of history in secular terms. He writes: "That is the mission of the proletariat: to bring forth supreme dignity from supreme humiliation. Through its sufferings and its struggles it is Christ in human form" (Camus, *Rebel*, 1956, 205). Of course, mockery is not philosophy, but Camus has more to say. His criticisms of Marx take three principal forms.

First, he criticizes Marx for mixing his methods. He claims that Marx uses scientific inquiry to study the workings of capitalism, dialectical reasoning to explain the progression of history, and prophecy to imagine an end to history. (Note: "the end of history" is the end of class divisions not the end of time.) If history were truly dialectical, Camus argues, it ought to continue its dialectical development, but Marx the prophet will not have it so. As Marx's predictions fail, Marx and his successors become more insistent on the earthly paradise that lies at the end of history.

Second, Camus criticizes Marx's economic determinism. According to Camus: "pure determinism is absurd in itself" (Camus, *Rebel*, 1956, 199). If it were not, Camus reasons, then one single affirmation would suffice to lead from consequence to consequence to the entire truth, and that chain of consequences has never been discovered. This is a poor argument, but it points again to Camus' failure to understand issues of free will and determinism.

Third, Camus criticizes Marx for ethical double-dealing. On the one hand, Marx scorns those who seek guidance from moral principles rather from economic realities. On the other hand, Marx treats the classless society as an end that justifies whatever means are employed to hasten its coming. Yet, as Camus suggests, being a historical end is not the same thing as being an ethical end. Whether one ought to hasten the coming of some future state of affairs will depend on

84

whether that state of affairs is good, and that requires independent principles of value. The equality of all citizens in a classless society cannot be good, unless equality is good. "The end of history," Camus writes, "is not an exemplary or a perfectionist value; it is an arbitrary and terroristic principle" (Camus, *Rebel*, 1956, 224).

From Marx, Camus passes to Lenin. He describes Lenin as a "mediocre philosopher" who scorns moral principles and "believes only in the revolution and the virtue of expediency" (Camus, *Rebel*, 1956, 226). Although Camus does not speak of Stalin by name, he portrays the totalitarian state created by Lenin and Stalin in uncompromising terms. He emphasizes the addiction of this state to servitude, terror, and world domination. Camus is particularly scathing in denouncing the hypocrisy of Soviet communism. "The dialectic miracle," he writes, "is the decision to call total servitude freedom" (Camus, *Rebel*, 1956, 234). On this point, he finds fascism less objectionable than communism. "The first represents the exaltation of the executioner by the executioner; the second, more dramatic in concept, the exaltation of the executioner by the victims" (Camus, *Rebel*, 1956, 246-247). Furthermore, he castigates Soviet communism for trying "to prove by means of its police, its trials, and its excommunications that there is no such thing as human nature" (Camus, *Rebel*, 1956, 250). Communism treats humankind as a product of economic forces, and in so doing fails to affirm "a limit, a dignity, and a beauty common to all men" (Camus, *Rebel*, 1956, 234).

This criticism is particularly important for it points the way to Camus' proposals for justifying morality and preventing rebellion from becoming tyranny. Until the mid-1940's, Camus had believed that without a God or supernatural order to validate the objectivity of moral values, morality was nothing but subjective preference. His experience in the French Resistance led him to challenge this nihilistic outlook and take a moral point of view. Yet it is not until *The Rebel* that Camus begins to come to grips with alternative possibilities for justifying moral objectivity. The justifications he proposes are incomplete and open to criticism, but they represent an advance in his philosophical thinking and provide a basis for linking the personal values that Camus found intuitively appealing with his recommendations for political actions. These justifications are based on Camus' new beliefs about human nature, communication, and cooperation.

In *The Rebel*, Camus claims that every human being desires freedom, dignity, beauty, and to give unity to his or her existence. He also asserts that there are principles of measure, limit, and moderation that are fundamental to human nature. He writes, for example:

> In history, as in psychology, rebellion is an irregular pendulum, which swings in an erratic arc because it is looking for its most perfect and profound rhythm. But its irregularity is not total: it functions around a pivot. Rebellion, at the same time that it suggests a nature common to all men, brings to light the measure and limit which are the very principle of this nature (Camus, *Rebel*, 1956, 294).

What Camus seems to mean is that while humans may experiment with a very wide range of personal values, life styles, and political systems, there is a much narrower range that leads to human fulfillment. When people stray too far—personally or politically—from what works for them as humans beings with a common nature, they end up generating less fulfilling lives. Thus, Camus reasons, that in order to make human lives as fulfilling as possible, we ought to promote rather than prevent freedom, dignity, beauty, and opportunities (e.g. sufficient leisure) to strive for unity in one's personal life.

To develop the social and political consequences of this view, Camus turns to communication and cooperation. He argues that the key to ethical behavior is "mutual recognition of a common destiny and the communication of men between themselves" (Camus, *Rebel*, 1956, 283). Indeed, he insists that any action or institution that obstructs mutual understanding and communications works against human fulfillment. Perhaps because of his background as a journalist, he lays particular stress on freedom of self-expression, honesty, and plain language. But he also advocates equality before the law, civil rights, fixed prison terms, and abolition of the death penalty. Above all, he declares that a society true to the spirit of rebellion must oppose servitude, falsehood, and terror.

Of course, Camus recognizes that no society can eliminate evil. "[C]hildren will still die unjustly even in a perfect society. Even by his greatest effort man can only propose to diminish arithmetically the sufferings of the world." (Camus, *Rebel*, 1956, 303). Therefore, we must be prepared to fight evil even at the cost of our own innocence. There are times, Camus admits, when even the right-minded rebel will be able to avoid killing or complicity in killing. The best he [or she] can do "is to work at diminishing the chances of murder . . . obstinately dragging the chains of murder, with which he is bound, toward the light of good. If he finally kills himself, he will accept death" (Camus, *Rebel*, 1956, 234).

Camus' proposal that justified killing should be atoned by suicide is probably the strangest idea in *The Rebel*, but it is not unintelligible. Moral men and women sometimes find themselves forced to choose the lesser of two evils. For example, members of the French Resistance who fought against the Nazis by blowing up trains sometimes caused the death of innocent people. It is understandable that Resistants who had blown up a train might feel guilty about the loss of innocent lives despite their confidence that they had acted morally. However, most ethicists would distinguish between *feeling* guilty and *being* guilty. They would argue that you cannot *be* guilty of wrongdoing if you have done the right thing, even though you may *feel* sorrow about some of the consequences of your action.

Why didn't Camus draw this distinction? I suspect there are two reasons. First, Camus was caught between *consequentialist* and *deontological* positions when it came to the morality of killing. (A consquentialist judges the rightness of an act by its consequences; a deontologist maintains that certain kinds of acts are always right or wrong.) Generally, Camus was a consequentialist, but his abhorrence of killing was so strong that he was drawn toward the view that killing is always wrong. Second, Camus' "Christian preoccupations" disposed him to deal with tough moral questions in terms of atonement and penance, despite his unwillingness to believe in God or an afterlife.

Six months after its publication, *The Rebel* was reviewed in Sartre's journal *Les Temps modernes* by one of Sartre's closest associates, Francis Jeanson. The review was nastier than either Sartre or Camus expected. Its title "*Camus ou l'âme révoltée*" mocked the title of Camus' book and suggested that Camus was a "shocked soul." The review praised *The Rebel*'s literary style but criticized its arguments as superficial and moralistic. Camus responded with a haughty and indignant letter addressed to "the editor" ("*Monsieur le directeur*"). Sartre struck back with a devastatingly personal reply addressed to "My dear Camus" ("*Mon cher Camus*").

In the course of his reply, Sartre accuses Camus of being conceited, preachy, arrogant, and moralistic—a judge rather than a writer. He assets that Camus detests difficulties of thought and avoids reading primary sources. He ask Camus to consider the possibility that *The Rebel* "simply attested to [his] philosophical ignorance," that it consisted of "hastily assembled and second-hand knowledge," "false reasoning," and "weak and confused ideas" (Sartre 1965, 81). Sartre praises Camus' earlier writings and actions, but accuses him of having lost touch with contemporary reality. "Your personality, alive and authentic as long as it was nourished by the event, became a mirage. In 1944, it was the future. In 1952, it is the past . . . ." (Sartre, 1965, 101). Sartre also charges Camus with being obsessed by his hatred of God: an "anti-theist" who wants to spit into the face of a blind and deaf God for the death of a child but ignores the economic injustices that may have contributed to that child's death.

With fifty years of hindsight, we can see that Camus had a clearer view of the Soviet Union's moral bankruptcy than Sartre. But in 1952, both men were trying very hard to see and say what was right at a muddy moment in history.

After this exchange of letters, Camus and Sartre never met again, but their differences multiplied. Sartre, surrounded by his "family" of followers, sought to unite Marxism with existentialism and sided with the FLN rebels who wanted to liberate Algeria from France. Camus, working in relative isolation, continued to oppose Marxism and supported a "civilian truce" between French and Arab Algerians. In 1954, Simone de Beauvoir published *The Mandarins*, a novel about the French intellectuals after the liberation of Paris. One of the novel's principal characters, Henri, is a satirical portrait of Camus. These events helped set the stage for Camus' next novel, *The Fall*.

E. Selfishness and Guilt: *The Fall*

The Fall (*La Chute*) was published in 1956, five years after *The Rebel*. Although Camus had planned to use it as one of the stories in *Exile and the Kingdom* (1957), it became too long. *The Fall* is a one-way conversation between a former lawyer from Paris and another middle-class man he meets in Amsterdam at a dockside bar frequented by sailors, pimps and thieves. It is not until the end of the novel that we discover that the other man is also a lawyer from Paris. The speaker introduces himself as Jean-Baptise Clamence (a false name), but we never hear the name of his interlocutor. The conversation continues over a period of five days: first in the bar, then along the canals, then on Marken Island in the dammed inlet known as the Zuider Zee, and finally at Clamence's apartment.

Except for talk and changes in locale, there is no significant action during these five days. Clamence "confesses" the sins of his life in an effort to seduce his interlocutor into doing the same. Selfish to the core but obsessed with guilt, Clamence has created the role of judge-penitent (*juge-pénitent*) to surmount his own sins by using them as bait to lure other sinners into self-judgment. He describes his moral weaknesses, hypocrisies, infidelities, and debauchery in order to create a mirror of vice in which the interlocutor can see his own face. The confessions of others make him feel "like God the Father" (Camus, *Fall* 1956, 143).

On one level, *The Fall* can be read as a satire on proud and gifted French intellectuals like Sartre and Camus. Although Clamence and his interlocutor are lawyers, the polished stories, arguments, and wordplay that flow from Calmence's lips sound more like the banter of writers in a Montparnasse café than the summations of lawyers in a courtroom. But which writer is he? Is Clamence more like Sartre or more like Camus? It is certainly possible to see Clamence as a reflection of Sartre, a moralizer and womanizer who was never at a loss for words, or as an exemplar of Sartre's incisive account of shame and pride in *Being and Nothingness* (1943) as two expressions of the same emotion. But I think Clamence has a deeper bond with the three main characters in Sartre's play *No Exit* (1944). Sartre's characters find themselves in a parlor in hell where they, the damned, makeup for a shortage of devils by serving as each other's psychological torturers. Similarly, Clamence is both damned and demon: a tormented soul who takes delight in tormenting others. Clamence compares Amsterdam's concentric canals to the circles of hell and tells his interlocutor: "we are in the last circle" (Camus, *Fall*, 1956, 14).

It is also possible to see Clamence as a reflection of Camus, the "virtuous" atheist who could never let go of Christian themes or be faithful to his wife. Although Camus knew that his wife Francine was tormented by his infidelities and that they were part of the reason for her suicide attempts, he continued not only to be unfaithful but also to appear in public with his mistresses. Like Clamence, Camus sometimes slept with the wives of his friends. When Camus showed Francine parts of his manuscript, she remarked: "You're always pleading the causes of all sorts of people, but do you ever hear the screams of people who are trying to reach you?" (Todd, 342). Camus once observed: "The little morality I know, I learned on the soccer field and the stage" (Todd, 354). Clamence admits "I have never been really sincere and enthusiastic except when I used to indulge in sport, and in the army, when I used to act in plays . . ." (Camus, *Fall*, 1991, 87-88).

A number of commentators, including Warren Tucker, André Abbou, Herbert Lottman, and Stephen Bronner, have suggested that Clamence is a grotesque caricature of the failings of which Sartre and his friends had accused Camus. Bronner explains it this way:

> Camus surely sought to exert his revenge on Sartre with this novel. What he had lost on the battlefield of philosophy, he now attempted to recover by fighting on a different terrain. . . . Sartre told Camus that he is poor no longer . . . so Clamence relinquishes all his possessions in order to live with the downtrodden. Sartre condemned Camus for removing himself from the struggle, so Clamence takes responsibility for everything. Sartre criticized Camus for his moralizing; so Clamence surrenders morality entirely (Bronner, 1999, 123).

How could a caricature of this kind serve to counter Sartre's accusations? It could do so in two ways. First, it could constitute an artistic *reductio ad absurdum* (the refutation of a premise by demonstrating that it leads to a logical contradiction or nonsense). Second, it could provide a mirror in which Sartre and his friends could see themselves.

Although this interpretation is attractive, it need not be regarded as exclusive. According to Camus' secretary, Suzanne Agnely, Camus began by modeling Clamence after himself and then broadened the character to make him more universal. A key to Camus' intent is the epigram which he borrowed from Mikhail Lermontov's *A Hero of Our Time*. That epigram concludes: "*A Hero of Our Time*, gentlemen, is in fact a portrait, but not of an individual; it is the aggregate of the vices of our whole generation in their fullest expression" (Camus, *Fall* 1956).

No doubt, Camus intended *The Fall* to portray the vices of his generation, but he also intended something universal. As its title suggests, this novel incorporates themes of original sin and the loss of innocence. Camus had always been interested in the question of why people do bad things, but he had previously avoided the Judeo-Christian tradition of putting the blame on depraved human nature. In *The Plague*, he put the blame on ignorance. In *The Rebel*, he had put the blame on bad ideologies. In *The Fall*, Camus suggests that human nature may be fundamentally flawed by selfishness.

Although Clamence is a cynical, dishonest, and sometimes destructive character, his misdeeds do not proceed from ignorance, error, or malice. He does not use and betray people because he fails to see that such conduct is wrong. Neither is he animated by misplaced religious or ideological convictions. He is not driven by metaphysical ideals like the prosecutor in *The Stranger*, the revolutionaries in *The Rebel*, or the missionary in "The Renegade." Neither does he display any inclination to harm or humiliate people for the sheer satisfaction of diminishing their lives or making them suffer. Clamence uses and betrays people because he is selfish.

It is important to note that the kind of selfishness (egoism) at issue here is *not* the inescapability of acting on the basis of one's own motives in the making of conscious choices. In this trivial sense, every choice I make is egoistic, since it is always *my* choice and always involves *my* motive for making that choice. Thus, if my conviction that it is wrong to enjoy a high standard of living while other people are starving leads me to give away most of what I own, it is still true that in acting in this way I am satisfying *my* moral conviction. But the selfishness at issue in *The Fall* is the egoism of serving one's self-interest at the expense of others. Clamence is eager to serve his own interests and wellbeing; he has no inclination to serve the interests or wellbeing of others. For Clamence, other people matter only to the extent they can be used as means to advance his ends.

The examples are manifold. In a German prison camp in North Africa, he repays his election as "pope" by drinking the water ration of a dying comrade. When he tries to achieve deeper fulfillment by falling in love, he finds he cannot do it. "For more than thirty years I had been in love exclusively with myself. What hope was there of losing such a habit? I didn't lose it . . . ." (Camus, *Fall* 1956, 100). Even when shame leads him to give up his property, he cannot bring himself to give it away. "Not being sufficiently big-hearted to share my wealth with a deserving poor man, I left it at the disposal of possible thieves" (Camus, *Fall* 1956, 128). He even fantasizes about a world in which other human beings would exist only when he wanted them to exist. "They must receive their life, sporadically, only at my bidding" (Camus, *Fall*, 1956, 68).

Clamence's unbridled selfishness may remind us of Meursault's indifference to the interests of others, but there are at least four critical differences. 1) Meursault worries very little about the judgments of other people, whereas Clamence has a horror of being judged. 2)

Meursault is a spontaneous sensualist who is content to live with great simplicity in the present, whereas Clamence is a greedy sensualist who is always fretting over the significance of his life as a whole. 3) Meursault feels himself a brother to "the gentle indifference of the world," whereas Clamence yearns for supernatural grace that will lift him above this world. 4) Meursault seems immune to feelings of guilt, whereas Clamence is obsessed with such feelings. The cumulative effect of these differences is to shine a spotlight on the problem of selfishness. Unlike Clamence and Meursault, Camus was not indifferent to the interests of others, but he recognized how often and easily he neglected the interests of others in pursuit of his own comfort, pleasure, and vanity. *The Fall* was a return to unfinished business.

Clamence's "fall," the event that cracks his façade of self-deception and exposes his selfishness, is a stock example among ethicists. It is the challenge of risking one's own life to save a drowning stranger. Walking across a bridge one rainy night in Paris, he passes a young woman staring into the Seine. Shortly after leaving the bridge, he hears a splash followed by cries—going down stream. "I wanted to run and yet didn't stir. . . . Then, slowly under the rain, I went away. I informed no one" (Camus, *Fall*, 1956, 70). In the days that follow, Clamence avoids reading the newspapers. He returns to his life as a successful attorney, who takes pride in helping blind people cross the street and defending criminals too poor to pay for a lawyer. Then, two or three years later, he hears laughter on the street behind him and his life begins to crumble. Others know his secret: his good deeds are merely devices for making himself look good. He discovers that people are laughing at him behind his back and judging him.

Clamence's problem is an extreme example of a common but philosophically interesting dilemma. His problem is that he feels guilty about his selfish behavior and would like to get rid of those guilt feelings, but he is unwilling or unable to change that behavior. Among the philosophical questions suggested by this problem are the following: 1) Is it wrong to be selfish? Or, more precisely, do I have a moral obligation to serve (promote or protect) the interests of other people when those interests are not advantageous to me? 2) If so, how much time, energy, wealth, risk, etc. should I devote to other people's interests? 3) Is it possible to become less selfish?

Philosophers differ greatly in the answer they have given to these questions. For example, Ayn Rand (1905-1982) argued that it is right, not wrong, to be selfish. For Rand, it would be immoral to risk one's life to save the life of a stranger who had foolishly thrown herself off a bridge, although it would be morally permissible to take personal risks during a public emergency in order to restore conditions necessary for normal life. Peter Singer (b. 1946), on other hand, has argued that if one can prevent something bad from happening to another person, without sacrificing something of comparable moral value, then it would be wrong not to do so. On the question of becoming more generous, Thomas Hobbes (1588-1679) claimed that our fundamental disposition to act on the basis of self-interest cannot be changed. Many philosophers have disagreed and reasoned that one's concern for the interests of others is a function of temperament, conditioning, education, and the cultivation of moral habits. Sartre held that free will made it possible for anyone to become more generous (even saintly), but argued that after age twelve or so this could only be accomplished by transforming one's entire way of being-in-the-world.

What are Camus answers? As usual, Camus lacks the philosophical background and vocabulary to formulate alternative possibilities with precision. Nevertheless, one would have expected him to try to reconcile the apparent conflict between Clamence's moral perversity and the ethical ideas suggested by Dr. Rieux. In *The Plague*. Rieux suggests that virtue and vice are primarily a function of one's moral knowledge or ignorance: people behave viciously because they are ignorant and virtuously because they know what they have to do. He says of the people who exposed themselves to greater risk by volunteering to work in the sanitary squads: "There was nothing admirable about this attitude; it was merely logical" (Camus, *Plague*, 1948, 122). But Clamence is a man who is obsessed with his own moral failings and yet cannot bring himself to correct those failings. It appears that Clamence's problem is weakness of will rather than lack of moral knowledge and, consequently, that his failure challenges the idea that one who knows the good will do the good.

But there are other possibilities as well. Perhaps the root of Clamence's problem is his isolation. Human beings seem to be capable of greater courage and selflessness or greater cruelty and vice when they are acting as part of a group. Perhaps the root of Clamence's problem is misplaced guilt. It could be argued that Clamence behaves like a scoundrel because he cannot bring himself to behave like a saint or hero. If Clamence had not felt so guilty about failing to dive into the cold waters of the Seine, he might have called for help instead of walking away. Unfortunately, Camus does not explore these possibilities. Instead, he turns to Christianity as a failed ideal against which to vent his discontent, or as Sartre would say, "to spit into the face of God."

Clamence is drawn to Christ because "he knew that he was not altogether innocent" (Camus, *Fall*, 1956, 113). This is Basilides again, but with a Biblical footnote. Clamence imagines Jesus suffering from the knowledge that his birth prompted Herod to slaughter the infants of Judea. But Clamence faults Christianity for abandoning Christ's three-year mission of guaranteeing innocence—"a huge laundering venture" (Camus, *Fall*, 1956, 111). He also faults it for transforming Christ, who asked us not to judge each other, into a universal judge. "I'll tell you a big secret," Clamence says, "Don't wait for the Last Judgment. It takes place everyday" (Camus, *Fall*, 1956, 111). Perhaps as a token of that secret, Clamence has installed in his cupboard a stolen panel from Jan van Eyck's altarpiece "The Adoration of the Lamb." The panel depicts "The Just Judges" arriving on horseback to adore the sacred lamb. But Clamence is no sacred lamb, and he does not find in Christianity absolution for incurable sinners like himself.

So Clamence becomes his own prophet—"an empty prophet for shabby times" (Camus, *Fall*, 1956, 117). His prophecy is empty because, unlike his namesake, John the Baptist, he has no messiah or good news to shout. ('*Clamans*' in Latin means 'he who shouts.') He closes his law practice in Paris, disposes of his possessions, and moves to the damp urban wilderness (or hell) of Amsterdam to play the role of judge-penitent. By pretending to be penitent, he gets others to confess, which permits him to pretend to sit in judgment and "feel like God the father" (Camus, *Fall*, 1956, 143). But Clamence is not blind to the superficiality of this game. "To be sure," he says, "my solution is not ideal. But when . . . you know that you must change lives, you don't have any choice, do you?" (Camus, *Fall*, 1956, 144).

The Fall ends on an interrogative note. Still haunted by his failure to save the young woman who jumped off the bridge, he wonders whether he would or could act differently if the moment were repeated. He dreams of a second chance—a chance to prove his goodness, or at least to preserve his illusion of goodness. "O young woman, throw yourself into the water again so that I may a second time have the chance of saving both of us!" (Camus, *Fall*, 1956, 147). But he is glad not to have to make that hard choice again. "Brr . . . ! The water's so cold! But let's not worry! It's too late now. It will always be too late. Fortunately!" (Camus, *Fall* 1956, 147).

F. After *The Fall*

It is fitting that *The Fall* ends on an interrogative note, for the novel as a whole is full of unanswered questions. For various reasons, some of them personal, Camus had started to wonder about an evil side to human nature. In *The Rebel*, Camus had looked to human nature as a foundation for morality. He had found innate desires for freedom, dignity, beauty and unity complemented by inborn principles of measure, limit, and moderation. In the mid-1950's, Camus had begun to find selfishness, mendacity, and cruelty as well. After *The Fall*, Camus worked on a number of projects, including his stage adaptations of Faulkner's *Requiem for a Nun* and Dostoyevsky's *The Possessed*, a collection of editorials and essays on Algeria entitled *Actuelles III*, an essay against capital punishment called *Reflections on the Guillotine*, and his novel *The First Man*. Each of these projects touched on evil.

In *The First Man*, for example, Camus tries to imagine how his father (presented here as Jacques Cormery) might have reacted to the atrocities he encountered in the Moroccan war in 1907 and 1908. After finding the bodies of French soldiers whose sexual organs had been cut off and stuffed in their mouths, Cormery tells his friend Levesque "a man doesn't let himself do that kind of thing!" (Camus *FM*, 1996, 65). When Levesque replies that Frenchman do it too, Cormery cries out: "A filthy race! What a race! All of them, all of them . . ." (Camus, *FM*, 1996, 66).

It is impossible to know where Camus' "interior adventure," his slowly maturing meditations, would have taken him. If Camus had been less preoccupied with flogging Christian theology or more interested in the useful distinctions available in philosophical ethics (Christian and non-Christian), his progress might have been swifter. But Camus was determined to chart his own course. Angry with Christianity and distrustful of philosophical reason, he sought to enlighten himself and his readers about what is good and bad in human life by patiently examining how people behave and how they attempt to give coherence to their lives. For guidance, he relied on his own intuitions, his skills as a writer, and the small philosophical vocabulary with which he felt comfortable. This was seldom philosophy in the professional sense of the term, but it was always an earnest search for wisdom.

BIBLIOGRAPHY

Standard Editions of Camus' Works in French

Camus, Albert. *Carnets*, ed. Roger Quilliot, Paris: Gallimard 1962, 1964, 1989.

_____. *Essais*, ed. Roger Quilliot, Paris: Gallimard, "Bibliothèque de la Pléiade," 1965. (*Essais*)

_____. *La Mort heureuse*, Cahiers Albert Camus, Paris: Gallimard, 1971.

_____. *Le Premier Homme*, Cahiers Albert Camus, Paris: Gallimard, 1994.

_____. *Théâtre, récits et nouvelles*, ed. Roger Quilliot, Paris:Gallimard, "Bibliothèque de la Pléiade," 1965. (*TRN*)

Standard Editions of Camus' Works in English

Camus, Albert. *Between Hell and Reason*, tr. Elisabeth Young-Bruehl, Hanover, NH, Wesleyan University Press, 1991.

_____. *Caligula and Three Other Plays*, tr. Stuart Gilbert, New York: Vintage, Alfred A. Knopf, 1958, reprint, New York: Vintage, 1962. (*CTOP*)

_____. *Exile and the Kingdom*, tr. Justin O'Brien, New York: Alfred A. Knopf, 1957, reprint, New York: Vintage, 1991. (*EK*)

_____. *The Fall*, tr. Justin O'Brien, New York: Alfred A. Knopf, 1956, reprint, New York: Vintage, 1991. (*Fall*).

_____. *The First Man*, tr. David Hapgood, New York: Alfred A.

Knopf, 1995, reprint, New York: Vintage, 1996. (*FM*)

_____. *A Happy Death*, tr. Richard Howard, New York: Alfred A. Knopf, 1972, reprint, New York: Vintage, 1995.

_____. *Lyrical and Critical Essays*, tr. Ellen C. Kennedy, New York: Alfred A. Knopf, 1968, reprint, New York: Vintage, 1970. (*LCE*)

_____. *The Myth of Sisyphus and Other Essays*, tr. Justin O'Brien, New York: Vintage, 1955. (*Myth*)

_____. *Neither Victims nor Executioners*, tr. Dwight MacDonald, Chicago, World Without War Publications, 1972.

_____. *Notebooks: 1935-1951*, tr. Philip Thody, New York: Alfred A. Knopf, 1965, reprint, New York: Marlowe & Company, 1998. (*N*)

_____. *The Plague*, tr. Stuart Gilbert, New York: Random House, 1948. (*Plague*)

_____. *The Possessed: A Play in Three Parts*, tr. Justin O'Brien, New York: Alfred A. Knopf, 1960, reprint, New York: Alfred A. Knopf, 1968.

_____. *The Rebel*, tr. Anthony Bower, New York: Alfred A. Knopf, 1957. (*Rebel*)

_____. *Reflections on the Guillotine*, tr. Richard Howard, Michigan City, Indiana: Fridtjof-Karla Publications, 1959.

_____. *Resistance, Rebellion, and Death*, tr. Justin O'Brien, New York: Alfred A. Knopf, 1960, reprint, New York: Vintage, 1995. (*RRD*)

_____. *The Stranger*, tr. Matthew Ward, New York: Alfred A. Knopf, 1988, reprint, New York: Vintage, 1989. (*Stranger*)

_____. *Youthful Writings*, tr. Ellen Conroy Kennedy, New York: Alfred A. Knopf, 1973, reprint, New York: Marlowe and Company, 1976.

Selected Biographies and Critical Studies

Amiot, Anne-Marie and Jean-Francois Mattei, *Albert Camus et la philosophie*, Paris: Presses Universitaires de France, 1997.

Archambault, Paul, *Camus' Hellenic Sources*, Chapel Hill: The University of North Carolina Press, 1972.

Brée, Germaine, *Camus and Sartre*, New York: Dell Publishing Co., Inc, 1972.

Brée, Germaine, *Camus*, New Brunswick: Rutgers University Press, 1959.

Brée, Germaine, ed., *Camus: A Collection of Critical Essays*, Englewood Cliffs: Prentice-Hall, Inc., 1962.

Bronner, Stephen Eric, *Camus: Portrait of a Moralist*, Minneapolis: University of Minnesota Press, 1999.

Cruickshank, John, *Albert Camus and the Literature of Revolt*, New York: Oxford University Press, 1959.

Davison, Ray, *Camus: The Challenge of Dostoevsky*, Exeter: University of Exeter Press, 1997.

Douglas, Kenneth, ed., *Albert Camus*, New Haven: Yale French Studies, 1960.

Hanna, Thomas, *The Thought and Art of Albert Camus*, Chicago: Gateway, 1958.

Judt, Tony, *The Burden of Responsibility: Blum, Camus, Aron, and the Twentieth French Twentieth Century*, Chicago: The University of Chicago Press, 1998.

Kamber, Gerald, "The Allegory of the Names in *L'Etranger*," *Modern Language Quarterly* Vol. 22, 1961, pp. 292-301.

Lottman, Herbert R, *Albert Camus: A Biography*, Garden City, NY: Doubleday & Company, 1979

McCarthy, Patrick, *Camus*, New York: Random House, 1982.

Onimus, Jean, *Albert Camus and Christianity*, tr. Emmett Parker, Alabama: University of Alabama Press, 1970.

Rhein, Phillip H., *Albert Camus*, Boston: Twayne Publishers, 1989.

Rizzuto, Anthony, *Camus' Imperial Vision*, Edwardsville: Southern Illinois University Press, 1981.

Sprintzen, David, *Camus: A Critical Examination*, Philadelphia: Temple University Press, 1988.

Todd, Oliver, *Albert Camus: A Life*, tr. Benjamin Ivry, New York: Alfred A. Knopf, 1997, reprint, New York: Carroll & Graf Publishers, Inc., 1996.

Willhoite, Fred H. Jr., *Beyond Nihilism: Albert Camus's Contribution to Political Thought*, Baton Rouge: Louisiana State University Press, 1968.

Wood, James, "The Sickness Unto Life," *The New Republic*, 8 November 1999, pp. 88-96.

Other Works Cited

Grouix, Pierre, "L'absence de la philosophie dans *Le premier homme*," in Amiot, Anne-Marie and Jean-Francois Mattei, *Albert Camus et la philosophie*, Paris: Presses Universitaires de France, 1997.

Nagal, Thomas, *Mortal Questions*, Cambridge: Cambridge University Press, 1979.

Nehamas, Alexander, *Nietzsche: Life as Literature*, Cambridge: Harvard University Press, 1985.

Nietzsche, Friedrich, *Beyond Good and Evil: Prelude to a Philosophy of the Future*, tr. Walter Kaufmann, New York: Vintage, 1989, reprint, New York: Random House, 1966.

_____. *Twilight of the Idols* in *The Portable Nietzsche*, tr. Walter Kaufmann, New York: Viking Press, 1955.

Pascal, Blaise, *Pensees*, New York: E. P. Dutton & Co., Inc., 1958.

Pascal, Blaise, *Pensees,* tr. A. J. Krailsheimer, New York: Penguin Group, 1966.

Sartre, Jean-Paul, *Literary Essays*, New York: Philosophical Library, Inc., 1957.

Sartre, Jean-Paul, *Situations*, tr. Benita Eisler, New York: George Braziller, Inc., 1965, reprint, New York: Editions Gallimard, 1964.